SAFER SANER SCHOOLS

Restorative Practices in Education

Ted Wachtel and Laura Mirsky, Editors

INTERNATIONAL INSTITUTE FOR RESTORATIVE PRACTICES
Bethlehem, Pennsylvania, USA

Safer Saner Schools
Restorative Practices in Education
Copyright © 2008
International Institute for Restorative Practices
All Rights Reserved
Printed in Canada

10 9 8 7 6 5 4 3 2 1
First Edition
International Institute for Restorative Practices
P.O. Box 229
Bethlehem, PA 18016 USA

Editors
Ted Wachtel and Laura Mirsky

Book and Cover Design
Christopher MacDonald

Library of Congress Control Number: 2008929485
ISBN-13: 978-1-934355-01-5
ISBN-10: 1-934355-01-1

Contents

All chapters in this book were originally published in the Restorative Practices eForum, an online publication of the International Institute for Restorative Practices, unless otherwise noted.

About the
Editors and Contributors

JOHN BOULTON has worked at Bessels Leigh School, in Abingdon, England, for 24 years, the last 14 as principal. Bessels Leigh is a residential special secondary school for up to 30 pupils who exhibit social, emotional and behavioral problems. Boulton first introduced restorative justice to the school in 2004, and thereafter embarked upon the process of changing the organizational culture by developing and using restorative practices. He became a Churchill Fellow in 2005 and used the opportunity provided by this travel award to observe different aspects of the IIRP organization in Pennsylvania.

DOUGLAS GRAVES is a freelance writer from Allentown, Pa. He received a B.A. in sociology from the University of Washington and an M.A. in human resources management from Pepperdine University.

DR. JEAN KANE is a senior lecturer in Educational Studies, University of Glasgow, Scotland. She works in the field of inclusive education with particular interests in social class and gender in education. She has been involved in national and locally-sponsored research projects in this field and has provided consultancy to local authorities seeking to develop more inclusive school provision. She has published widely in books, journals and government reports.

DR. GWYNEDD LLOYD is an honorary fellow at the Moray House School of Education, University of Edinburgh, Scotland. Her professional interests include inclusion and exclusion, education and social welfare policy, law and young people's rights, the construction and use of labels and categories of deviance, and the identification and development of supportive professional practice with young people in difficulty in and out of school. She has published widely in books and journals on restorative approaches and education.

DR. GILLEAN MCCLUSKEY is a lecturer at the Moray House School of Education, University of Edinburgh, Scotland. Her work concerns restorative approaches, exclusion from school, discipline and behavior management in schools, the connections between excluded pupils and the general population, group work with young people and education for marginalized groups. She has published several articles and reports in journals and on behalf of the Scottish government.

LAURA MIRSKY, editor, is communications coordinator for the International Institute for Restorative Practices, where she edits and sometimes writes for the Restorative Practices eForum and produces other print and video resources. She has been a newspaper reporter and columnist and has worked in book publishing, film, television and advertising.

ABBEY J. PORTER is a Philadelphia-based writer with a background in journalism and academic and nonprofit communications. She has worked as a freelancer for the International Institute for Restorative Practices and for regional Pennsylvania magazines. She also works in the public relations office of The Wistar Institute.

NANCY RIESTENBERG is a prevention specialist for the Minnesota Department of Education (MDE) and provides consulting services on violence and bullying prevention, school connectedness, cultural relevance of prevention education, crisis prevention and recovery and restorative measures. She provided technical assistance to the Minnesota school districts that experienced school shooting incidents and serves as the MDE staff member to the Minnesota School Safety Center. She helped design the "Restorative Measures: Respecting Everyone's Ability to Resolve Problems" program and the National Institute of Corrections' restorative conferencing curriculum for law enforcement and school personnel. She has written several articles on restorative measures in schools.

DR. SHEILA RIDDELL is professor of Inclusion and Diversity, and director of the Centre for Research in Education Inclusion and Diversity, the Moray House School of Education, University of Edinburgh, Scotland. Her work addresses inclusion and diversity, equality and human rights and lifelong learning. Her publications include numerous books, book chapters, journal articles, conference papers and government reports.

DR. JOAN STEAD is a researcher at the Moray House School of Education, University of Edinburgh, Scotland. Her research interests include inclusion and exclusion, restorative practices in education, ADHD and qualitative methodologies. She has published many journal articles and government reports on these topics.

JOSHUA WACHTEL is the son of IIRP founding president Ted Wachtel and Community Service Foundation and Buxmont Academy (CSF Buxmont) co-founder Susan Wachtel. He attended a CSF Buxmont school as a senior in high school and taught history and music at CSF Buxmont for four years. He currently resides in western Massachusetts and contributes regularly to the Restorative Practices eForum.

TED WACHTEL, editor, is president and founder of the International Institute for Restorative Practices (IIRP), a graduate school in Bethlehem, Pennsylvania. He also presides over the IIRP's Training and Consulting Division, which provides restorative practices training throughout the world, as well as print and video resources and international conferences. In 1977, Wachtel founded Community Service Foundation and Buxmont Academy, which operate schools, foster group homes and other programs in Pennsylvania — demonstration programs for the use of restorative practices with delinquent and at-risk youth. Wachtel's publications include the books *Toughlove*, for parents of troubled adolescents, *Real Justice* and *The Conferencing Handbook*, about restorative conferencing, as well as numerous book chapters and journal articles.

DR. ELISABET WEEDON is deputy director of the
Centre for Research in Education Inclusion and Diversity,
the Moray House School of Education, University of
Edinburgh, Scotland. She has published numerous book
chapters, journal articles and government reports.

LYNN M. WELDEN currently authors eForum articles for the
IIRP and implements marketing projects for the Institute. She has
been an author, critic and managing editor of a regional magazine
and has worked in a range of corporate and nonprofit venues.

FOREWORD

Schools everywhere in the world are faced with increasingly challenging behavior among their students. The new field of "restorative practices" not only provides solutions for effectively addressing misbehavior, but guides educators in creating a more positive school community.

Proactively, restorative practices improves relationships and communication among students, parents, teachers and administrators. When wrongdoing occurs, instead of simply doling out punishment, schools use restorative practices to engage students and truly hold them accountable. Directly involving the wrongdoers in repairing the harm they have caused and in restoring relationships they have damaged fosters a sense of responsibility and empathy. Empathy creates understanding and respect for others and therefore is the key to changing behavior.

Research at schools where restorative practices has been implemented reveals dramatic declines in offending behavior and disciplinary problems, along with remarkable improvements in student attitudes.

The International Institute for Restorative Practices is a graduate school that offers master's degree programs for educators and other children-and-youth-serving professionals. The IIRP also provides on-site training and consulting throughout the world and publishes internet and print resources, produces films and organizes international conferences.

Allow the vision of hope described in this anthology to move you from thought to action. It's an exciting time for anyone ready to take the next step in improving human relations, and I invite you to join our global effort to "restore community in an increasingly disconnected world."

You may subscribe without cost to our Restorative Practices eForum, which published the articles in this book and regularly publishes articles like it on the internet, by signing up at our website (iirp.org). You may directly support the solutions we offer by contributing to the Restorative Practices Foundation (restorativepracticesfoundation.org), which underwrites training and consulting for disadvantaged communities and developing countries and provides scholarships for graduate students.

The world needs our vision of hope.

Ted Wachtel
President
International Institute for Restorative Practices

1

Restoring Community
in a Disconnected World

*The Inaugural Address of the IIRP Graduate School
Founding President*

*Ted Wachtel was inaugurated as president of the International Institute for
Restorative Practices Graduate School in a ceremony on October 8, 2007,
in Bethlehem, Pennsylvania, USA, where the school is located.*

BY TED WACHTEL

Thirty years ago my wife Susan and I, both public
school teachers, were looking for solutions to the
increasingly challenging behavior of young people in schools, families and communities. We left public
education, founded the first of several nonprofit organizations and developed schools, group homes and other
programs for delinquent and at-risk youth. As time went
on we realized that the successful strategies we were using with the troubled young people in our programs had
implications for all young people, and for adults as well.

We and our colleagues also got involved with an innovative approach in the field of criminal justice, called
"restorative justice," which provides opportunities for
victims, offenders and their family and friends to meet

and, to the extent possible, repair the harm caused by a crime. This development in criminal justice, giving people an opportunity to express their feelings and ideas and have a say in resolving the conflict, matched parallel developments in other fields.

Primary school educators were using talking circles and morning meetings to improve classroom climate, secondary educators were adapting restorative justice to address discipline problems, social workers were organizing family group conferences to bring together extended families to solve problems of abuse and delinquency involving their own loved ones, and business managers were using horizontal management strategies to empower their employees to solve problems in the workplace.

Known by different terminology, all of these developments share a common premise: that people are happier, more cooperative, more productive and more likely to make positive changes when those in authority do things *with* them rather than *to* them or *for* them. This premise is part of a unifying conceptual framework that helps to explain human motivation and social behavior, from families and classrooms to workplaces and communities.

Building on the momentum of the restorative justice movement, we decided to name this emerging transdisciplinary field of study "restorative practices." We conducted research in restorative practices, provided trainings, produced videos, published articles and books, created websites and organized international conferences.

In 2000 we incorporated the nonprofit International Institute for Restorative Practices, the IIRP, to consolidate all of our research and educational activities. In

2006 the Pennsylvania Department of Education authorized the IIRP as a degree-granting graduate school, and in doing so, recognized restorative practices as a field worthy of graduate study. During that six-year effort from incorporation to authorization, only those who climbed the mountain with us can fully appreciate how steep the slope, how disappointing the setbacks and stumbles, and how joyous it was when we finally reached the summit.

> We must find ways to adapt and to compensate for our profound loss of social connectedness. And I know that restorative practices can play a critical role in doing just that — in restoring community and fostering relationships in an increasingly disconnected world.

But the journey ahead will be even more arduous. We must now thoughtfully re-examine and change many of the practices that govern how our modern societies run schools, administer justice, organize welfare systems, manage workplaces and even how we raise children.

I'm a pragmatist. If it's working, then why change it? But it's not working. Most people seem to share a growing concern that things in general are not going well.

We are living in an unprecedented social experiment. We have systematically changed the patterns and connections that have characterized human life as long as there has been human life. Never before in the history of the human race have so many lived so far from their extended families. Never before have so many lived outside of traditional neighborhoods in which all the adults served as the collective parents of each other's children. Never before have so many marriages ended in divorce and divided families. Never before have so many elderly grown older among the elderly in unfamiliar surroundings. Never before have so many children left their hometowns for other places.

These developments have reduced our social capital — the relationships and the connectedness that bind people together and create a sense of community.

From the founding of the United States, when more than 90 percent of us worked on farms to less than 3 percent of us at present, technology has transformed our nation and our world. My 92-year-old father, who is here today in the audience, remembers the crackling sounds of the first radio broadcasts, the first refrigerators, the first commercial airlines, and, as a soldier expecting to participate in the invasion of Japan, the first use of nuclear weapons. Driven by technological change, family farms, neighborhood stores and local factories have given way to agribusiness, national discount store chains, fast-food franchises and multinational corporations. Globalization and the relentless growth of government have dramatically altered our lives.

William Irwin Thompson wrote, "At the edge of history the future is blowing wildly in our faces, sometimes brightening the air and sometimes blinding us." He said, "In straining our industrial technology to the limit, we have, in fact, reached the limit of that very technology. Now as we stand in the shadow of our success, there remains light enough to see that we are approaching a climax in human cultural evolution."

I'm not a doomsday prophet and I know that we cannot turn back the clock. Rather, we must find ways to adapt and to compensate for our profound loss of social connectedness. And I know that restorative practices can play a critical role in doing just that — in restoring community and fostering relationships in an increasingly disconnected world. But to do so, we are going to have to re-examine why we do things the way we do them.

A boy gets angry, curses at his teacher, and she sends him to the assistant principal, who suspends him from school for three days. This kind of occurrence is commonplace in schools today. We lament the lack of civility, the loss of behavioral boundaries, the irresponsible parents who have raised this child, and we explain the punishment as "holding the student accountable for his behavior."

Accountable? How so? The punishment is passive. The student doesn't have to do anything. He stays angry with

Ted Wachtel gives his inauguration speech, applauded by George South-worth, representing the University of Pennsylvania, and Dr. Vivian Nix-Early, dean of Campolo School for Social Change of Eastern University.

the teacher and the assistant principal. He thinks he's the victim. He doesn't think about how he's affected others or about how he might make things right. And he returns to the classroom with nothing resolved.

Nils Christie, the distinguished Norwegian criminologist, wrote a landmark essay entitled "Conflict as Property." He argued that our conflicts belong to us and that courts and lawyers steal our conflicts, taking away our opportunity to resolve them and robbing us of whatever benefits might come from that. Schools and administrators do the same.

Both courts and schools miss a critical opportunity for people to resolve things with better results.

The restorative justice movement was founded by people who were experimenting with meetings between victims and offenders to negotiate restitution agreements. They learned that the encounter was more important than the restitution — that both victims and offenders valued the opportunity to talk to each other and resolve their conflict.

I was speaking about restorative conferencing to an audience in Philadelphia when a woman from Africa said, "What you're describing is exactly what my father would do. As a chief, he would always bring everyone together to deal with a crime or a conflict."

Bonnie George of the Wet'suwet'en First Nation in British Columbia was a plenary speaker at the IIRP World Conference, in Vancouver, Canada, in 2004. She contrasted her people's indigenous justice system with the adversarial Western system in which strangers make decisions on behalf of others, without emotional involvement. She said, "With our system, because of our relationships and our kinships, we're all connected to each other one way or another, and those are the people that are making the decisions. Our goal is to restore balance and harmony within the community." So if restorative practices is the wave of the future, we may take comfort in knowing that it is also as old as the hills.

If the assistant principal wanted to ensure the angry student would return appropriately to that teacher's classroom, he would organize a restorative conference to bring the offending student and his family together with the teacher and other students who were affected by the incident. Although it may surprise those unfamiliar with restorative conferencing, such meetings almost always produce positive outcomes, allowing the student and teacher to be restored to balance and harmony.

There is a growing body of research supporting the use of restorative practices. In schools, restorative practices reduces disciplinary incidents and improves school climate. In our own demonstration programs run by the Community Service Foundation and Buxmont Academy, empirical research found a particularly impressive outcome — those delinquent and at-risk youth who spent three months or more in our restorative milieu were half as likely to offend.

So we have created the IIRP Graduate School, and it has three critical roles. The first, of course, is education. We offer master's degrees to help educators, youth counselors and other professionals meet the challenge of today's world, because all too many have been prepared for a world that no longer exists. The fact that we now teach about restorative practices at the most advanced level of professional development will benefit not only our own graduate students, but will influence other institutions of higher education to pay attention to this new discipline. The second role is research. We will strive to

The founding faculty of the International Institute for Restorative Practices (from left): Margaret Murray, librarian; Beth Rodman, professor; Dr. Patrick McDonough, vice president for academic affairs; Dr. Paul McCold, professor; Dr. Tom Simek, professor; Carolyn Olivett, professor; and Dr. Frida Rundell, professor.

meet the highest standards of scientific inquiry. And the third role is communication. We will generously share the exciting potential of restorative practices with others so that all of us may collaboratively change the world.

I say, "change the world" unabashedly. We must not be embarrassed by our optimism. Who could have imagined 30 years ago that we would be educating probation officers in Romania, police in Iceland, law professors in Costa Rica, child care workers in South Africa, prosecutors in Jamaica and educators in Hong Kong? Or that our educational efforts would assist the Thai Ministry of Justice in carrying out more than 17,000 restorative conferences diverting young people from incarceration?

The first master's degree class (June 2008) of the International Institute for Restorative Practices (from left): Christine Meyers, David Suesz, Julie Vitale, John Bailie, Jolene Head, Steve Orrison, Pam Thompson, Craig Adamson, Elizabeth Smull, John Infantino, MaryLynn LaSalvia-Keyte and Samantha Heyman. Not pictured: Judy Happ, Paul Langston-Daley.

Or that Hull, England, a city of a quarter-million, would be using our programs to educate 23,000 social workers, educators and others serving children and young people to create the world's first restorative city? Or that I would be standing here today, accepting responsibility for leading the world's first graduate school wholly dedicated to restorative practices?

So don't let the naysayers get you down. The world needs our vision of hope. The human race now holds in its mortal hands the power to tinker with the genetic underpinnings of life, to alter the climate of our planet, to extinguish whole species, and to wield, as weaponry, the awesome energy of the stars. Our technological skills have outpaced our social skills, but restorative practices can correct that imbalance.

No, we are not pursuing an unrealistic utopian dream. We recognize that conflict is integral to being human. What we propose, however, is to get better at managing conflict. And to minimize conflict by proactively restoring community in an increasingly disconnected world.

2

A Day at
a CSF Buxmont School

"Welcome to CSF!"

BY LAURA MIRSKY

I began my day at an 8 a.m. staff meeting, and was warmly welcomed by Mark, the staff coordinator, and the counselors, who seemed like a dedicated and enthusiastic group of (mostly) young people. As the day went on, I would see just how dedicated they were. I then set about to be a fly on the wall. It was to be a rather unusual day for the school, but I had no inkling of that yet.

It was the last two weeks of school and "the natives were restless," as one counselor put it. Arrangements were discussed for the big school picnic planned for the next day. To complicate matters, half of the staff was to leave for a meeting in the afternoon. There was talk of drug testing: One student had reported using marijuana the week before.

I went with Shaun to the "downstairs community's" morning circle meeting. (I would later learn that the school was divided into two communities — the downstairs and the upstairs — for a total of about 75 kids, in

grades 7 through 12.) The downstairs community was ready for the meeting, sitting in chairs in a circle, when Shaun and I arrived. No staff member had told them to do this. They had taken the initiative upon themselves, apparently as a matter of course. I found this impressive, as I knew these kids had been sent there because they had been labeled "problems" by their school district or the courts. Looking around the circle, the kids appeared to represent a wide range — racially, socially and in terms of age and maturity.

There was an atmosphere of happy bustle in the room. "Good morning," said Shaun to the kids. "Good morning, Shaun!" the kids sang back. I took a seat outside the circle and the kids immediately asked me to pull my chair into it, implying, "There are no outsiders here." Right off the bat I felt welcomed by the group, and it felt good. Sitting in the circle, I could no longer feel like a fly on the wall. Looking back on it, I realize how smart this welcoming ritual is. It's a mechanism by which newcomers to the school are not left to feel like outsiders, as so many of them must feel in the outside world.

The meeting began with the questions: "Any problems? Announcements?" — not from Shaun, the counselor, as I expected, but from the kids. This was no fluke, I would learn as the day wore on, but central to the school's philosophy, and indicative of how kids at CSF are asked to take responsibility for themselves. I could see that what was happening here was different from the routine at other schools. How many schools begin the day with kids of all ages meeting in a circle to discuss what's on their minds?

Just then my eyes were caught by a poster on the wall entitled "How Do You Feel?" illustrated with drawings of faces depicting different emotions: "Bored, Frustrated, Confident, Joyful ..." I saw many of the emotions pictured on the poster reflected on the faces of the kids in the circle and realized that this was a place where they were encouraged to feel, name, own and understand their emotions.

In the meeting, some kids seemed to stand out naturally as leaders, and they did much of the talking and questioning of the other kids. "People need to start bringing stuff in for the picnic," said one girl. Another answered, "I live in a group home so I can only bring one thing." With that comment, I got my first inkling of what some of the kids' lives must be like.

The kids now called for introductions, I assume because a stranger was in their midst — me. We went around the circle and everyone said his or her name, age and where they were from. Kids displayed varying degrees of alertness and sleepiness, affect and lack thereof, some mumbling, some voluble — just like any other group of teenagers, perhaps, except that here a higher than usual number said that they lived in group homes.

I introduced myself and was greeted with applause and a hearty group "Welcome to CSF!" I was surprised at how much this moved me. Again, I would realize that this was all part of the wise welcoming ritual.

There followed a brief discussion of the school's "cardinal rules" which seemed to be for the benefit of the new kids in school. Kids can arrive at CSF at any time of year, depending on the circumstances that brought them. Again, the request for this discussion came from kids concerned about their fellow students.

There are five cardinal rules that students learn when they're given an orientation packet on arrival.

1. No drug or alcohol use.
2. No stealing.
3. No violence or threats of violence to people or property.
4. No leaving school premises without permission.
5. No sexual activity.

A girl now asked a new boy: "What does R.C. mean?" He tried hard to articulate an answer: "When they're doing something wrong and you find out, and they don't tell anybody, and if you don't tell anybody you'll get in trouble, too."

In the orientation packet are a few paragraphs entitled "Responsible Concern," by Donald J. Ottenberg, M.D., which include the following: "If I'm lying to myself or others — tell me... and if I'm not strong enough to take it to my group and counselor,

you take it there for me. That will be an act of courage and an act of love."

The new boy had focused on what would happen to him — he'd "get in trouble" — if he didn't practice responsible concern. He apparently hadn't been a part of the community long enough yet to understand how he would benefit from the practice, or how he would help others. But — because the other kids were asking him to — he was trying to get it, and that in itself was remarkable to witness.

Some "side conversations" began to pop up in the group — kids talking among themselves. Counselor Jay, who had recently joined the circle, now asked, a bit sternly, "Do we need to go over the norms, or what?" It seemed that even something as relatively minor as talking out of turn during the circle meeting was very important in the world of the school, not out of some arbitrary concept of discipline, but to maintain a steady structure in these kids' otherwise chaotic lives.

(The "group norms," decided by the group as a whole, include things like: No side conversations, Confront appropriately, No sleeping, Be caring and Participate.)

Time was now called for the end of the meeting, and the kids — without being told — automatically transformed the room from a meeting place, with chairs in a circle, into a classroom, with tables and chairs set up for learning.

A personable young man of about 13 now took me on a tour of the school. "We set up our classes ourselves," he told me, confirming what I'd just seen. I asked how the classes were divided up in terms of grades. He said that all grades learned together in each class — be it math, science, English, social studies, music, art or industrial arts: "individual learning," he called it.

In English class, for instance, they had writing assignments, time lines and vocabulary. In social studies they were learning about the Great Depression. They stayed longer in their classes here than they do in public school — 45 minutes as opposed to 35. But, he said, here he didn't pay attention to time the way he did in public school. He also told me that here kids helped with school maintenance.

> Here, kids weren't being punished for their behavior. They had come from systems where that had been tried and hadn't worked. Instead, they had come to a place that provided both control and support in equal measure. They were learning a concrete way to talk about and deal with their problems, with the help of their fellow classmates and staff members.

My tour guide now dropped me off with Bob Costello, director of training for the International Institute for Restorative Practices, who gave me a thorough overview of the CSF organization, including its history and philosophy. Community Service Foundation was started in 1977 by public school teachers Ted and Susan Wachtel as a school for kids who were having trouble at public school. Now it is three separate organizations that work together: the Community Service Foundation, Buxmont Academy and the International Institute for Restorative Practices. Eight schools, all called Community Service Foundation (CSF) or Buxmont Academy by the kids, in Bucks, Montgomery, Northampton and Delaware counties, are licensed by the state of Pennsylvania as private academic schools, as well as providers of drug-and-alcohol and behavioral counseling.

There is not a lot of emphasis on whether fellow classmates were sent there by the courts or by their school district, said Bob, adding, "It's one big family." They stay from several months to years, depending on "who's paying and what the issues were" that brought them. The organization also has a residential program of 16 foster group homes. All the programs have been "remarkably successful with difficult kids," said Bob.

We got into the theory behind restorative practices — the philosophy behind all the schools and programs. When there is high control and low support of kids the result is punitive. In that model, when punishment fails, the solution is to punish harder. At the opposite extreme — high support and low control — the outcome is permissive. Both are disrespectful of kids. The ideal is to provide both high control and high support at the same time, the outcome being restorative. "This doesn't mean no consequences, or that people always like what happens to them," said Bob, "but they have a say." It's "communitarian," he concluded. Bob told me that they've taken restorative practices techniques to public schools with the SaferSanerSchools program. "We have this dream that we'll put ourselves out of business," he said.

"What happens if a kid is found with drugs at school?" I asked. First, he said, they ask the kid what happened, and if the presence of drugs is confirmed, police are notified. "We ask the kid who has been affected by what he has done and what he needs to do to make things right," said Bob. In a group, the child makes an announcement of what he has done and gets feedback. Then he is asked to make a plan to ensure it doesn't happen again. "What they do is up to them," said Bob. "That's why it works."

I now went to observe an English class. Kids sat at tables working on vocabulary assignments or making time lines for a movie they'd watched, "The Education of Little Tree." Judy, the teacher, circulated, helping kids in turn. After a while she addressed the class, warning, "There's far too much in the way of side conversation going on here." A little later, she announced, "If it gets any louder, we're going into a group." A few minutes after that, Judy had the class pull their chairs into a circle for a discussion and asked what was going on.

"I was confronting," said one boy. "I was talking," said a few other children. "It annoyed Judy that I was talking," said another. "I was cursing," said yet another. "When people confront and they're doing the same thing they're telling other people not to do, they're being hypocritical," commented one girl. "What does this do to the class?" asked Judy. "It breaks up the class," came the response. Judy then asked for "a quick go-around about what each of you will try to do to make it better." The replies: "Do my work and get it all done."

"Sit there and be quiet." "Not get mad and swear at people." "Do my work and listen to my teacher." "How about you, Judy?" asked one boy. "I'm going to try to keep my class focused," she promised.

I had just heard a boy ask his teacher what she was going to do to help make her class function better. She had not gotten angry, accused him of being a smart aleck, or threatened punishment, but had openly and honestly replied to his question. Clearly, not just counselors, but teachers here also employed restorative practices techniques.

As it turned out, a little later in the day the entire school was called together into one big group. I didn't witness the reasons for this unusual occurrence, but I heard that several arguments had broken out in two or three classes at once. I did sit in on the big group meeting.

One boy suggested that everyone in the circle "take ownership" for what they had done to cause the problems leading to the meltdown. "I called X a thief." "I swore at X." "I refused to put down any tables." "I was confronting people inappropriately." "I didn't confront or support." "I blew off (counselor) Jay," ... said the kids.

Mark, the staff coordinator, now addressed the group, saying he was very disappointed. "It's never been this chaotic," he told them, and it made him sad and hurt. But, he said, he wasn't going to sit there and scream. "I look around this room," he said, "and at least 75 percent of the kids do what they need to do and say what they need to say." He said that several people were repeatedly having problems. He encouraged them not to come to school, if they didn't want to be there. But, he said, "If you want to end [the year] successfully, you're welcome."

Tracy, a counselor who was pregnant, told the group that in the last few days "people have been hurting me so bad." She was afraid, she said, because she was "responsible for an unborn human being." She continued, "I know you because you're a student that gets sent here, but I care about you because you deserve to be cared about. ... This is your chance to take control. ... Make your choice or it will be made for you."

After the meeting was over, I saw one of the boys who had been acting up apologize to Tracy, saying he felt very bad for hurting her. He said he knew how wrong it was because his girlfriend was pregnant too. It seemed very important to him that Tracy accept his apology. It didn't appear that he was just going through the motions for effect. "Your body language was very threatening," Tracy told him, making sure to give him feedback about his behavior.

Later I asked the staff what they thought had caused so many problems that day. Restlessness and fear about the imminent end of the school year was the consensus.

After lunch I attended a group feedback session, a structured process whereby kids passed a ball around and commented openly to each other, one at a time. I found this extremely moving: "When you help other people I feel proud of you." "When you take a leadership position I feel confident you'll do a good job." "When you treat me like a human being I feel good because not that many people treat me like a human being." "When you rush me I feel frustrated." Each piece of feedback got a reply, none of which, to my amazement, was defensive: "I'm sorry." "Thank you."

I was also amazed to see that the group made sure that everyone got to give and get feedback, that nobody was left out. These kids clearly cared about each other very much. I was really beginning to see how restorative practices worked.

I now interviewed several students one-on-one, asking them how they had come to the school and what it had done for them. One boy, 16, said that he had been at the school for two years. He had been "acting up" at his old school and got caught with drugs and a gun. CSF had helped him, he said, because it "changed my anger" and taught him to accept the consequences of his actions. "When you get in trouble here," he said, "you get to bring it up in group, make anger plans." Next year he was going back to public school and hoped to graduate and get a job in construction. "I'm ready," he said. "I know right from wrong. I know what I gotta do." There are better things in life than "the streets," he added. The most helpful thing he had learned? "Not to let people get me angry. I'll just talk about it instead."

Another boy, 14, had been at CSF since January and loved it. He'd been out of control at his old school, but here, he said, "If one of my friends confronts me, I stop." "I used to run around and beat up stuff with baseball bats," he said. "Now I've figured out I can take care of my stuff and seek positive attention."

A 16-year-old girl told me she had been at the school for nine months. Before that she hadn't been to school in six years. "I got into drugs and alcohol — whatever I could get my hands on," she said. "In the beginning I hated it here," she admitted, but now she liked it. She had learned that she was an alcoholic and took part in an intensive CSF after-school program. She lived in a CSF group home, spending weekends with her family.

She had been clean for two months, having relapsed at six months. "My father is an alcoholic," she said, "And I turned to it to hide my feelings."

She said that she had received a great deal of support at CSF, but no "negative attention," something she had previously sought out. "I started being positive and I've been getting praise up and down," she said. She was studying for her G.E.D. [high-school equivalency test] with a CSF tutor and hoped to go on to community college. Restorative practices had helped her get along better with her family and "respect myself, most of all," she said, adding, "They told me nobody can love me until I love myself."

Another girl, 17, told me that she had been at CSF for a little over a year. She had been in juvenile detention and was on probation for truancy, bringing a weapon (an X-Acto knife) and "a little bag of weed that wasn't mine" to school. She had been in a group home but now lived at home again. She liked it at CSF because she felt safe and always had someone to talk to. She didn't want to go back to public school, although that was what seemed to be planned for her. She was afraid she would be behind when she got back. But she definitely wanted to go to college, adding, "I'm very serious. I want to be all I can be."

Asked how CSF was different from juvenile detention, she said, "All I gained there was weight." Detention had made her worse — "more pissed off; it gave me an 'F the world' attitude." Then she went to a group home where she was "breathing and eating CSF for 10 months." She still got mad, she said, but now she cared about things — her friends, her family, her future. "I didn't even pay attention that I had a future," she said, "Not even two minutes later, not even tomorrow." Now, she said, she was "a totally different person."

I interviewed a few more kids. Only one said she wasn't happy at CSF. She hadn't been there very long and seemed to be having a hard time of it. She lived in a group home, where they checked her for drugs all the time. She said that she had changed a lot, and that she was "not touching drugs and not fighting." She blamed other kids for the fact that "my name keeps coming up in a lot of stuff." She was upset that things weren't working out at CSF, but wished she were home with her mother. She had been given a choice: to sign and fulfill a "behavior contract" enabling her to stay or to leave. She wasn't sure which she would do, but she hadn't made the decision to leave. It seemed there was hope for her yet.

At the end of the school day, I attended a staff meeting where the counselors discussed what had happened that day in depth. "If the kids only knew how everything they said and did is analyzed, what would they think?" wondered one staff member. I brought up what I had noticed about the way certain kids seemed to be natural leaders. A counselor had an interesting response: "A lot of the kids who end up being leaders — their leadership qualities are what got them in trouble, but it's the same thing that can get them out of trouble."

I had spent a whole day at CSF watching classes, circles, groups, feedback sessions and staff meetings and interviewing kids, many of whom seemed to have been on a collision course with disaster. Who knows what might have happened to them if they hadn't been assigned to this place, where people not only cared about them but had figured out a specific, structured way to help them change their destructive — and self-destructive — behavior?

Here, kids weren't being punished for their behavior. They had come from systems where that had been tried and hadn't worked. Instead, they had come to a place that provided both control and support in equal measure. They were learning a concrete way to talk about and deal with their problems, with the help of their fellow classmates and staff members.

Above all, I felt that these kids were very lucky to have ended up at CSF. They were learning that, no matter where and what they had come from, they themselves were the only ones who were really responsible for their lives and able to change them for the better. How many of us never realize that?

3

Graduation
at a CSF Buxmont School
···
A Triumphant Step into the Future

By Laura Mirsky

On June 12, 2006, all the Community Service Foundation Buxmont Academy (CSF Buxmont) alternative schools held their graduation ceremonies. I attended one at the CSF Buxmont Woodlyn Center. This was no ordinary graduation, and CSF Buxmont schools are not ordinary schools. The Woodlyn Center, one of eight CSF Buxmont schools located throughout eastern Pennsylvania, USA, serves youth in grades 7 to 12 who, for one reason or another, are having trouble in other schools. These students have been referred to CSF Buxmont by their former schools or probation or children-and-youth departments, but the students themselves have made a commitment to come to CSF Buxmont and work on whatever brought them there in the first place. (CSF and Buxmont Academy are demonstration programs and sister organizations of the International Institute for Restorative Practices.)

At CSF Buxmont Woodlyn Center's graduation, about 60 friends and family members gathered to see three young men graduate and 21 other young people receive certificates of completion, honoring the number of successful days they'd spent at the school. To the strains of "Pomp and Circumstance," Woodlyn's staff of counselors, teachers and tutors filed into the room, followed by the students — the graduates in caps and gowns.

"At CSF Buxmont there are no suspensions," Woodlyn's coordinator, Jen Barvitskie, told the crowd in her graduation address. Instead, she explained, students are expected to participate as community members and respond to and offer feedback to each other. "Students are more likely to listen to each other," she said.

Barvitskie was describing the approach that guides all CSF Buxmont schools, foster group homes and drug-and-alcohol and supervision programs for youth. Called "restorative practices," the approach aims to enhance relationships by engaging people in participatory learning and decision making. Staff empower youth to take responsibility for their own behavior, make decisions, solve problems and support one another in their personal growth.

Restorative practices has made a difference in the lives of many thousands of adolescents who have participated in CSF Buxmont's programs since its first school was founded in Sellersville, Pennsylvania, in 1977. Formal research, which was presented to the American Society of Criminology, confirmed this difference, showing positive outcomes for youth who participated in the "restorative milieu" of CSF Buxmont schools, in three areas: lower offending rates, high program completion rates and posi-

tive changes in attitude. This 1999-2001 study was replicated in 2001-2003. (See Chapter 19, Research Reveals
Power of Restorative Practices in Schools.)

What I saw on June 12 at CSF
Buxmont in Woodlyn backed up that
research in a very concrete way. Here
are brief stories of the three young
men I saw graduate that day.

Curtis, 18, said he got into trouble
at his old school for fighting with kids
in rival gangs, but at CSF Buxmont he
decided to "do what he needed to do." Fighting, he says
now, is "stupid." At CSF Buxmont, he focused on his
schoolwork (math is his best subject) and took part in
groups where he learned to express himself, even though
that was hard for him. He did it, he said, for his mom
and his girlfriend. Now he wants to go to school to become an architect. He plans to build himself a big house
with an indoor basketball court.

Curtis's mom, April, cried as she presented him with his
diploma during the graduation ceremony. "I'm so proud
of my son today," she said. "He had a hard time coming
up. But now he goes to church, he plays the trombone.
He wants to be an architect. I'm proud my son made it,
and I love him." Later, she said, "CSF helped Curtis get
out of his shyness and make the right choices. Now he
lets me know his feelings."

Ken, also 18, said he used to have trouble controlling
his anger and communicating his feelings. He used to
threaten people, and he "had a lot of suspensions." Since
coming to CSF, he said, he doesn't lash out at people
anymore. He discovered that he likes to write songs and

> Restorative practices
> aims to enhance
> relationships by
> engaging people in
> participatory learning
> and decision making.

to work on computers. He learned to communicate to his peers, his counselors and his parents. He's looking forward to going to college, working on computers and joining the Navy. He feels good inside, he said, because he's accomplished something.

As Ken's mom, Joan, presented him with his diploma, she said, "I'm so proud of Ken. It was hard but we made it through. I love you." Ken's smile was dazzling as he held up his diploma, posing for pictures. Afterward, Ken's stepfather, Richard, said, "His whole attitude has changed. Now he discusses his problems instead of acting out in anger."

Ken, a jubilant graduate of CSF Buxmont, poses with his family.

Warren, 17, said he got in trouble at his old school for spraying a fire extinguisher. He described his former self as shy and nervous, angry, uptight and arrogant. At CSF Buxmont, he learned that if he had a problem, he could get it off his chest and feel better. He even joined the student council and became "the second boss of the school," responsible for organizing field trips and the school store. Now he's happy and excited to be graduating, something he's "been waiting for half my life." He's looking forward to working on his music and going to community college or joining the Navy.

Warren's mother, Lana, presented him with his diploma, saying, "I'm so proud of you, son. You've come a long way. You were mean and hateful, but now you're shining. Keep shining! I love you so much!"

Later, Warren's father said that when Warren first started at CSF Buxmont, he was isolated and didn't want to talk, had poor grades, a bad temper and no regard for authority. "I used to try to discipline him and whip him," he said. "It made him worse." Now, he said, "He's a good kid. And he takes a leadership position. He's got a lot of respect for people and his grades are all As and Bs." Added his mom, "I used to try to comfort him. Now he hugs me and says, 'I love you.' And he's funny!"

On June 12, 2006, at CSF Buxmont, three young men — angry and defiant "tough kids" who once could find no way out of the sorry trap they'd gotten themselves into — made their first triumphant steps into the future.

4

Transforming School Culture
with Restorative Practices

By Laura Mirsky

Twelve-year-old Tiffany (not her real name) rushes into the student office at Palisades Middle School, in southeastern Pennsylvania, USA. "Hi Tiffany," says the office secretary, Karen Urbanowicz, "What are you doing here?" Tiffany says that she was getting in trouble in class. Mrs. Urbanowicz asks Tiffany what happened and Tiffany tells her story. "Did your teacher send you here?" asks Mrs. Urbanowicz. "No," says Tiffany, "I sent myself." "Good for you!" says Mrs. Urbanowicz. She takes Tiffany's personal journal out of a file and hands it to her, saying, "Write about what happened and what you think you can do better in the future." Tiffany sits down and begins to write.

What made Tiffany feel comfortable enough to refer herself to the student office? How did the office secretary know what to do when Tiffany showed up? The school was introduced to restorative practices, through the SaferSanerSchools program.

SaferSanerSchools, a program of the International Institute for Restorative Practices (IIRP), a graduate school and training organization based in Bethlehem, Pennsylvania, was developed in response to a perceived crisis in American education and in society as a whole. Said Ted Wachtel, IIRP founder and president, "Rising truancy and dropout rates, increasing disciplinary problems, violence and even mass murders plague American schools. The IIRP believes that the dramatic change in behavior among young people is largely the result of the loss of connectedness and community in modern society. Schools themselves have become larger, more impersonal institutions, and educators feel less connected to the families whose children they teach."

A classroom circle at Springfield Township High School, Pennsylvania.

The IIRP was created to be the training and education arm of its sister organization, the Community Service Foundation (CSF). CSF was founded in 1977 by Ted and Susan Wachtel, teachers who left the public school system with a dream of building a different type of educational community. Over three decades, the private, nonprofit schools that they created have evolved strategies to work with the toughest adjudicated delinquent and at-risk kids in southeastern Pennsylvania. These methods developed by way of trial and error — out of necessity, not ideology.

The name they gave to these strategies is "restorative practices." Restorative practices involves changing relationships by engaging people: doing things WITH them, rather than TO them or FOR them — providing both high control and high support at the same time. Said Ted Wachtel, "In our schools, we provide a huge amount of support. We're very understanding and find all sorts of ways to help kids understand their behavior, but at the same time we don't tolerate inappropriate behavior. We really hold them accountable."

Instead of zero tolerance and authoritarian punishment, restorative practices places responsibility on students themselves, using a collaborative response to wrongdoing. Students are encouraged to both give and ask for support and are responsible for helping to address behavior in other students. This fosters a strong sense of community as well as a strong sense of safety. "Restorative practices is not a new 'tool for your toolbox,' but represents a fundamental change in the nature of relationships in schools. It is the relationships, not specific strategies, that bring about meaningful change," said Bob Costello, IIRP director of training.

Eventually the IIRP began to articulate these practices and find ways to teach them to others. They also found that the processes applied to many settings, not just with troubled kids. Since restorative practices worked so well with the toughest kids in their own schools, the IIRP thought they ought to be able to work in other schools as well.

Through a SaferSanerSchools pilot program, restorative practices has been introduced to Palisades High School (732 students), Palisades Middle School (559 students) and Springfield Township High School (855 students). All have implemented restorative practices in creative ways.

A visitor walking the hallways at any of these schools feels immediately welcomed into a lively and cheerful community. Ask any student for directions and he or she provides them in a spirit of open friendliness. Staff members seem just as congenial. An observer in classrooms and at special events perceives that students have a strong connection to their school, the staff and each other.

Palisades High School was the first SaferSanerSchools pilot school. Asked how restorative practices has changed the school, principal David Piperato said that before the program was introduced, as in many public schools throughout the U.S., the level of caring and respect among many students had declined. Restorative practices, he said, "created a more positive relationship between staff and students." Preliminary data gathered by the school indicate a clear decrease in disciplinary referrals to the student office (Figure 1), administrative detentions (Figure 2), detentions assigned by teachers (Figure 3), incidents of disruptive behavior (Figure 4) and out-of-school suspensions (Figure 5) from school year 1998-1999 through 2001-2002, the years of the pilot project.

Restorative practices also helped establish a culture of collaboration among staff members. Said teacher Heather Horn, "The traditional mind-set of, 'If you're

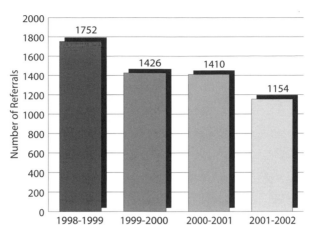

Figure 1. Palisades High School disciplinary referrals to student office.

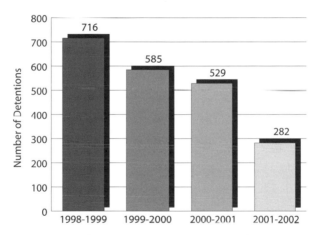

Figure 2. Palisades High School administrative detentions.

doing something wrong, it's not my job to confront you' has become, 'This is a team thing and your behavior is affecting me as a teacher.'" The administrator-teacher relationship is now collaborative rather than just supervisory, said Piperato: "the right style for a high school." Restorative practices has also had a positive effect on academic performance, he said, adding, "You cannot separate behavior from academics. When students feel good and safe and have solid relationships with teachers, their academic performance improves."

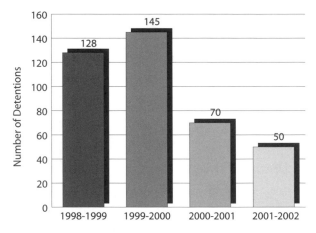

Figure 3. Palisades High School detentions assigned by teachers.

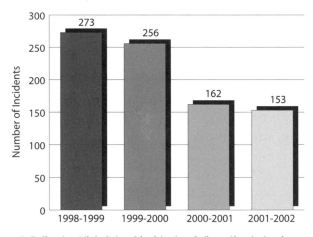

Figure 4. Palisades High School incidents of disruptive behavior.

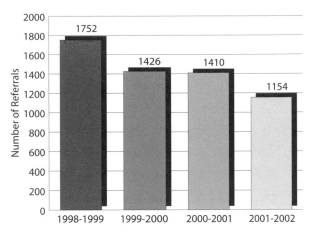

Figure 5. Palisades High School disciplinary referrals to student office.

Restorative practices was introduced at Palisades High School in the 1998-1999 school year. In the fall, the school had launched a new program, the Academy, for students who didn't feel connected to school and were struggling with behavior or academic performance. The Academy is project-based. Kids work with clients outside school to design websites, produce videos and build construction projects. But, said Piperato, "We made a critical error: We addressed the content of the program, not relationships between teachers and students. And from the first day, the program was as close to a disaster as you can imagine." Rebelling against the lack of structure, unmotivated kids roamed the building, their behavior rude and belligerent. Teachers turned on each other, frustrated and upset.

At that time, the IIRP presented their idea of implementing restorative practices in schools to Joseph Roy, then Palisades High School principal, and Piperato, then assistant principal. Roy and Piperato realized that they could use the IIRP's assistance with the Academy immediately. Said Piperato, "This was an opportunity for them to test their theory in our most difficult setting."

> "When you solve problems *with* students rather than coming down from 'on high' they buy into it much better."
>
> — Fran Ostrosky

Piperato said he knew that he and Roy needed to be intimately involved with the experiment from the beginning — supportive and willing to take risks. "The IIRP staff spent hours listening to us, gave us strategies for dealing with the kids and held us accountable for using them," he said. They started to see some success with the way the teachers were feeling almost immediately. The biggest step, said Costello, was when the teachers recognized that they had to take care of themselves as a team before they could help the kids. "They needed to respect their style differences, be honest, practice what they preached and work on their issues: do all the things they were asking the kids to do."

The IIRP taught the Academy staff to use the continuum of restorative practices, starting with affective statements and questions — sharing and eliciting emotion — to help students understand that they were as responsible for the success of the Academy, as well as to and for each other, as the teachers were, said Piperato. The teachers also learned how to use circles, interventions, one-on-ones and group meetings with kids. They introduced "check-in" and "check-out" circles at the beginning and end of each 90-minute class period — an opportunity for students to set goals and expectations together.

The strategies quickly started to show results with students. "Restorative practices helped us help students see that they need to buy into the community that we're building," said Academy teacher Eileen Wickard. Comments from Academy students indicate a strong sense of community: "We're a big family. We're all so different but we all work together." "If two people are arguing, a group of us will get together and talk to the people and try to work it through. As a group, we've managed to make ourselves more mature."

"You cannot separate behavior from academics. When students feel good and safe and have solid relationships with teachers, their academic performance improves."

— David Piperato

Word soon spread throughout the school that the Academy had been successful with students no one had been able to reach before. Academy kids were also receiving positive recognition from the community. Teachers in the rest of the school consequently became more willing to listen to the "wacky touchy-feely stuff going on in the Academy," said Piperato. Roy and Piperato decided to phase in restorative practices in the rest of the building over a three-year period. They divided the staff into thirds: the "believers," the "fence sitters" and the "critics." The first year, the IIRP provided basic knowledge of restorative practices for the believers, teaching them to be a support group for each other. "That was phenomenal for us," said Horn. Teachers used to complain to each other about kids and judge them, she said. But the IIRP taught teachers how to discuss students' behavior, rather than their personalities, and brainstorm as a group about how to handle it. "Before, it was almost a taboo," said Academy teacher John Venner. "You never talked to another teacher about how they talked to kids. It was their own damn business in their own classroom. Now we find it very acceptable to hold each other accountable."

> "I used to be one of these black-and-white, law-and-order guys. Kids had to be held accountable and the only way to do that was to kick them out of school. That doesn't work. Restorative practices works. We now fix and solve problems."
>
> — Edward Baumgartner

By the second year, said Piperato, the fence sitters had begun to notice the positive effects of restorative practices. The believers and the fence sitters were combined into two mixed groups, and the IIRP trained them together. The believers modeled, provided support and told stories about their experiences with restorative practices and the fence sitters learned from them. By the third year, teachers who needed evidence that the program worked were seeing it. Those who had been resistant were less so and many teachers retired. Newly hired teachers were trained with the third group. All teachers were encouraged to use restorative practices in the classroom.

English teacher Mandy Miller said that she uses restorative practices, including circles, to build relationships between students. She told a story of a girl who felt that other students were getting in the way of her learning and asked for a circle meeting to address the issue. During the circle, the girl realized that she was actually causing most of the problem herself. "That was a really hard day and people were in tears," said Miller, but since then, the entire class has been getting along fine. Miller has also found restorative practices helpful with discipline problems. "I can say, 'This is how I'm feeling. How are you feeling? And what are we going to do to work together?'" Students seem to value and understand the processes. A ninth-grade girl commented, "We do fun team-building activities in biology class to learn how to work with people you're normally not used to working with."

"The teachers respect us and we respect them back. They talk with us instead of at us."

— Senior, Springfield Township High School

Assistant principal Richard Heffernan said that in 2001-2002 they saw an increase in "harassing types of behavior," not high-level incidents, but those that were creating problems nonetheless. Said Heffernan, "We asked the IIRP staff, 'Why do you think this is happening? We're supposed to have restorative practices, express our feelings, treat people with respect and be responsible for our actions.' They said the reason we'd seen this increase was that students were reporting it more, because we had created a safe environment." The culture of the students as a whole had changed. It had become acceptable to "tell" when another student was making them feel unsafe. Added guidance counselor Monica Losinno, "Kids feel safe reporting it because they believe it will be addressed."

Heffernan and Losinno devised a program whereby a staff member is available every period of the school day

"We get along here, and that's because the kids are respected and they know it."

— Edward Baumgartner

to facilitate conflict resolution in a restorative manner. Eight teachers and teaching assistants received IIRP group facilitator training. When a problem arises, one of the eight talks with each of the students involved, then brings them together to help them work it through. Teacher and "conflict resolution manager" Richard Kressly said that the entire school staff was educated in restorative practices and asked to be more present in the hallways and more diligent about low-level incidents. The program does not relieve teachers from handling disruptive situations in class, said Heffernan.

Kids seem to appreciate the ways in which restorative practices has created a congenial climate in their school. Said a ninth-grade boy, "If kids get in a fight they have someone to help them work it out." A ninth-grade girl added, "We don't get many fights. I think there's only been two all year. That's not many at all for a high school. Most people get along real well." A 10th-grade girl who had transferred from another school said of Palisades High School, "One thing I noticed right way was the friendly atmosphere."

Restorative practices came to Palisades Middle School (PALMS) in the fall of 2000. Said Palisades Middle School principal Edward Baumgartner, "When I took over here two-and-a-half years ago, we were suspending

200 students a school year for everything from disrespect to not making up gym." The school climate was discourteous and disrespectful and altercations were common, he said, adding, "The behavior was the result of treatment, perceived or actual, in many cases. You've got to give respect to get it." Then, said Baumgartner, "I sat on the stage for graduation at Palisades High School in June of 2000 and saw a phenomenon that I didn't understand: Kids that had routinely been behavior problems at the middle school were hugging the assistant principal and thanking her." Baumgartner learned that the high school had implemented the SaferSanerSchools program and decided to follow suit at PALMS.

"Two-and-a-half years later," he said, "everybody in this building's been trained, including all the support staff. It's changed the way we teach kids; it's changed the way we think about discipline and behavior management. We get along here, and that's because the kids are respected and they know it." And, said Baumgartner, "We've seen a statistically significant decrease in the amount of actual problems that occur each and every day." Data gathered by PALMS indicate a substantial drop from school year 2000-2001 to 2001-2002 in discipline refer-

> "When you get to the point where your use of restorative practices is informal but constant, that's where you want to be."
>
> — Kevin McGeehan

rals to the student office (Figure 6), discipline referrals by source — teacher, cafeteria and bus company (Figure 7) — and in incidents of fighting (Figure 8).

In addition, there has been a significant increase in students reporting other students for behavior problems,

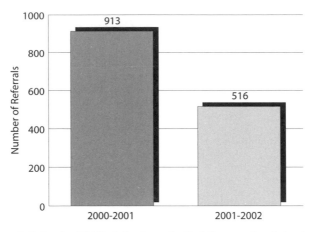

Figure 6. Palisades Middle School yearly disciplinary referrals to student office.

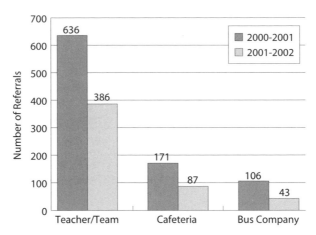

Figure 7. Palisades Middle School disciplinary referrals by source.

students self-reporting and parents reporting their children. Kids feel comfortable saying, "I've got a problem; I need help," said Baumgartner. Also, he said, "The school cafeteria is a place where I'm real proud of

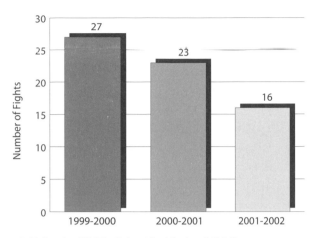

Figure 8. Palisades Middle School incidents of fighting.

the kids, a place that I would invite board members to come in and sit down every day."

"I've had an epiphany, a metamorphosis," said Baumgartner. "I used to be one of these black-and-white, law-and-order guys. Kids had to be held accountable and the only way to do that was to kick them out of school — to show the other kids that you're the boss. That doesn't work," he said. "I didn't solve problems; I just postponed them until they got to high school and then somebody else had to deal with them. Restorative practices works. We now fix and solve problems."

Asked if restorative practices has had a positive effect on academic performance, Baumgartner said, "Kids can't learn in a dysfunctional environment. If the teacher is spending valuable instructional time addressing a student who's acting out, that detracts from the instruction. If teachers can be more focused on instruction, the answer to your question has to be yes. We've gone down 400 classroom referrals, so I know that the answer is yes."

Palisades Middle School dean of students Dennis Gluck is also the intervention specialist — someone to facilitate restorative circles and model restorative practices for others. Gluck helped the IIRP implement restorative practices at PALMS. First, he said, the school identified six or seven kids who were really struggling and set up a restorative classroom with them. "It was really successful," said Gluck. "It showed the rest of the staff that this could work with the toughest kids in the school. The kids not only did well, but were able to help other kids." The whole staff then got excited about the possibilities of restorative practices, he said.

Restorative practices is used in classrooms in the form of circles, when kids and staff share information and problems. In discipline situations, kids can write in their personal journals, kept in the student office, about what happened and suggest how to take care of it. "Through that we process what would be appropriate, from an informal plan to a formal plan to a restorative conference," said Gluck.

Gluck said that they put a lot of thought into the processes that they developed. "We created a cafeteria committee to deal with problems, we had kids help other kids when they were in jams, and at the end of the year, some of the kids that had struggled the most went on the P.A. [public address] system saying that they loved the administrators."

Staff members appear enthusiastic about restorative practices. Veteran PALMS educational assistant Karen Bedics said that she has seen a big change in the students due to the approach. "Students at this age are very self-centered. They need a constant reminder that other people are affected by what they do. If we have a conflict, we will meet as a group and tell what part each of us, including the teachers, played in it. I'm not afraid to tell them my feelings and I always keep their feelings in mind," she said. Also, said Bedics, kids now "reprimand each other if they mess up. It means more to them to hear it from their peers."

Fran Ostrosky, longtime PALMS teacher and president of the Palisades Education Association (the teachers' union), said, "I've gotten more out of my students with this approach than I did with a more rigid approach to discipline problems. When you solve problems with them rather than coming down from 'on high' they buy into it much better."

Disciplinary aide Gretchen Carr said that restorative practices has "made a tremendous impact on these kids, in their behavior, in their respect for one another and the adults. It also helps that everybody in this district has adapted to it and is practicing the same thing," said Carr. "It's not going away and the kids realize that."

Kids seem to welcome the approach. "I used to get in a lot of trouble, but teachers talk to students and help you make the right decisions here. In homeroom we sit in a circle and talk about anything that needs to be brought up," said an eighth-grade girl. Said a seventh-grade boy, "When I disrespected a teacher and I apologized to her, it felt good. If they feel bad it'll make you feel bad too." An eighth-grade girl said, "The school has gotten to be a really nice community and people really treat each other fairly now."

District administrators are thoroughly supportive of SaferSanerSchools. "Restorative practices works," said

"Usually kids will catch onto 'OK, this is how we behave at this school, this is what the expectations are and this is the culture' and they get on board."

— Joseph Roy

Palisades School District superintendent Francis Barnes. "It requires a certain level of self-discipline from all of our staff and they have accepted that challenge and the students have responded very well." Said assistant superintendent Marilyn Miller, "Consistently what we hear from people who visit the schools from the outside is that our students are confident, happy and articulate. That was not the case in 1998."

After helping to implement restorative practices at Palisades High School, Joseph Roy became principal of Springfield Township High School in January of 2000. His strategy for introducing restorative practices at Springfield has been to "start with a small group and then do another small group and start to expand critical mass." He picked a few teachers he thought would be interested in restorative practices training, then a few more. "We're still at the beginning of the process here," said Roy.

Specific groups have been trained, including those working with poorly motivated, at-risk students in the Spartan Project, an American studies class that combines English and social studies, as well as teams of eighth- and ninth-grade teachers. Roy finds that the teaming concept is consistent with restorative practices. The entire faculty was introduced to restorative practices in the fall of 2001. "The goal," said Roy, "is to integrate the practices throughout the school. Our challenge here is changing the traditional school culture to become more restorative." Roy considers restorative practices to be "one piece of many things we do for culture-building," including treating kids with respect and having a team of teachers and parents identify the school's core values. "I guess you could tie it all in to restorative practices," he concluded.

The demographics at Springfield are different from those at Palisades, said Roy. "We're in the first ring of suburbs around Philadelphia," he said, "so we have a lot of transfer-ins from families moving to the suburbs for the better schools. These kids are much more city street smart than suburban kids. That's part of the challenge — to take kids that are coming from a different system and have them be integrated into the culture of this school and not have the culture of this school shift toward the behavior of the Philadelphia schools." Roy said that restorative practices had definitely helped with that concern. "Usually kids will catch onto 'OK, this is how we behave at this school, this is what the expectations are and this is the culture' and they get on board," he said.

The number of discipline referrals is down dramatically already since he came to Springfield, Roy said. Data gathered by the school indicates decreases in incidents of inappropriate behavior (Figure 9), disrespect to teachers (Figure 10) and classroom disruption (Figure 11). Added

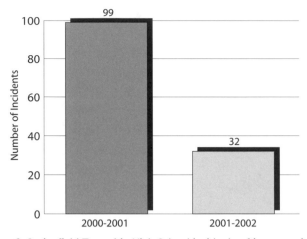

Figure 9. Springfield Township High School incidents of inappropriate behavior.

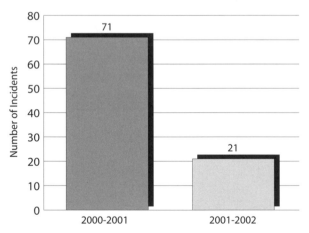

Figure 10. Springfield Township High School incidents of disrespect to teachers.

Roy, "They're lower-level stuff: Johnny didn't come back to study hall after he went to the library — stuff like that." In the past, said Roy, there were many more incidents of disrespect and defiance.

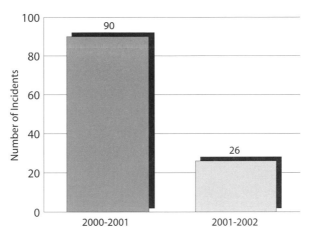

Figure 11. Springfield Township High School incidents of classroom disruption.

Said Roy, "When I first got here there was something called 'time-out.' Teachers would kick kids out of class and send them to a 'time-out room.' Sometimes they'd get there, sometimes they wouldn't. If they got there they just hung out. There was no follow-up. We put an end to that. Now, not nearly as many kids get kicked out of class, and if they do they come to our in-school suspension room and teachers are required to follow up and to contact the parents."

Now, instead of just "hanging out," said assistant principal Michael Kell, during in-school suspensions, a student is given a list of seven questions to think about along the lines of those asked in a restorative conference, i.e., What happened? Who do you think has been affected by your actions? What can you do to repair the harm? Kell discusses the questions with the student, sometimes bringing in the teacher involved as well. He asks both to talk about how they feel and helps them mend their relationship.

Kell is an enthusiastic proponent of restorative practices. "Usually the assistant principal — the chief disciplinarian — sets the tone for the building, and in that tone we've tried to create a restorative culture here," he said. He also works with teachers to help them be more restorative and trust the practices instead of simply blaming kids for problems. "One teacher thought we were lowering his authority in the classroom by using circles," said Kell. "I told him, 'I felt bad that you felt that I wasn't supporting you. You have the ability as a teacher to say how you're going to change things. Think of it as an investment. You're going to get dividends in the future.'"

Kell facilitates formal restorative conferences when serious problems arise. One conference brought a school custodian together with students who had been disrespectful to him. The custodian told the kids how they had hurt him and that he felt great pride in his work. The kids apologized to him and had new respect for him after the conference.

Guidance counselor Kevin McGeehan also facilitates restorative conferences. He ran a conference after members of an athletic team scratched their names into some new lockers during a school renovation. Chuck Inman, facilities director, who participated in the conference, was very impressed with the process, saying, "The kids got to realize that their actions had affected more people than they thought — their teammates, the construction workers and the taxpayers. The incident represented $900 worth of damage — a tiny fraction of the $27,000,000 school renovation — but "it was the principle that was important," said Inman. As a consequence of their actions, the kids had to pay to replace the locker doors.

McGeehan also uses a restorative approach in everyday interaction with kids. "When I see a kid acting up in the hallway, instead of immediately dragging him into the discipline office, I'll pull him over, one-on-one, and try to find out exactly what's happening and to understand where he's coming from," he said. "A lot of times it's not the specific incident that's caused the conflict, but rather something that's happened earlier in the day or at home or in a previous class. Allowing that venting process alone tends to diffuse it, along with the feeling that an adult is listening and understanding." Said Roy, "When you get to the point where it's informal but constant, that's where you want to be."

Roy encourages teachers to use the check-in and check-out model with both classroom management and academic issues to "create the culture that says, 'We talk about stuff as a group and we help each other out.'" Eighth-grade teacher Michele Mazurek uses check-ins on Mondays and check-outs on Fridays "to get a sense of community within the classroom." Just doing it twice a week has cut down on the number of incidents of teasing because students have heard each other relate some of their goals and aspirations, she said. A 12th-grade girl said that check-ins were "a way for people to open up and share what's important to them, then somebody else might relate to it. So people can relate to each other in ways they might not have."

Social studies teacher Dave Gerber was skeptical about the restorative practices training at first but is now an enthusiastic proponent of the approach. "My students know that I treat them with genuine respect, and I think that's where restorative practices begins and what really helps it take shape in the classroom," he said. A 12th-grade girl agreed, saying, "The teachers respect us and we respect them back. They talk with us instead of at us."

Palisades Middle School dean of students Dennis Gluck leads a circle.

Gerber said that it's possible to use restorative practices regardless of class level or content. In response to teachers who say they don't have time to implement the approach, he said, "You don't have to spend 40 minutes doing a circle. You can spend five minutes and it is effective. You'll be able to go back next class and make up for that five minutes of content you didn't get in. If you have people arguing in the classroom all the time, what kind of learning is taking place?"

Students at Springfield Township High School seem to appreciate their school's climate. A 12th-grade girl said, "Everybody accepts everybody for who they are. Our teachers are awesome. I try and do my best just so I can be like, 'I'm from Springfield, this is what they've taught me; this is what I'm doing; I'm going places in life.' I have that feeling. I think the majority of our school does, too."

Administrators and teachers at the three pilot schools believe that more needs to be done to continue to implement restorative practices in their buildings, but all feel that they have a solid foundation on which to build. Palisades High School teacher Heather Horn talked about the difficulties at the beginning of school year 2002-2003, due to contractual problems and a threatened teachers' strike (which never materialized) as well as a building torn apart by construction. Despite the turmoil, said Horn, there was a willingness to work toward repairing the climate among the entire staff, adding, "The effects of restorative behavior were clearer last fall than ever before."

Staff members at Palisades High School, Palisades Middle School and Springfield Township High School know that their education in restorative practices will be ongoing. To cite one example, Joseph Roy said that Bob Costello, IIRP director of training, scheduled to help Springfield implement a restorative practices-based program for the eighth grade. Time will be set aside for kids and teachers to break into small groups that will focus on goal-setting, community-building and academic issues. As Palisades High School principal David Piperato said, "Learning to be restorative is a lifelong process."

5

Restorative Practices
at Community Prep High School
New York City

BY LAURA MIRSKY

The International Institute for Restorative Practices (IIRP), via its SaferSanerSchools program, is providing training and consulting at Community Prep High School, a public school in New York City for young people just out of juvenile detention. These are the kind of kids who are typically stigmatized as "tough" or "incorrigible" and written off. The story of how the IIRP and Community Prep's staff collaborated to implement restorative practices at this remarkable school was reported in *The New York Times*, which we quote and summarize in this article.

"Each year, as many as 8,000 New York City students, ages 13 to 18, return to their neighborhoods from juvenile detention centers and placement facilities ... after serving time for offenses ranging from assault to drug possession. ... An overwhelming majority are black or Hispanic, and poor. They have low reading scores, records of truancy and disruptive behavior and few credits toward graduation. About half have been labeled as needing special education. Many have no parents at home," wrote Sara Rimer, in her article, "Last Chance High," *The New York Times*, July 25, 2004. "But just at this crucial moment, many high schools, reluctant to take on what they perceive as difficult students, turn them away."

Community Prep was launched in the fall of 2002 to help such students. The school is a partnership of CASES (the Center for Alternative Sentencing and Employment Services, www.cases.org), a nonprofit agency that operates programs in New York City, and the City Board of Education.

"The first year at Community Prep ... was rocky," wrote Rimer in the *Times*. "Teachers, who offered more support than structure, were overwhelmed."

CASES director Ana Bermúdez told the eForum, "Before we began our work with the IIRP, outrageous behavior and sporadic attendance were the norm at Community Prep. It did not feel like a safe place to be, much less a place for young people to turn their lives around."

> "Restorative practices helped Community Prep High School become a safe community, a place where students can make real, meaningful changes in their lives."
>
> — Mark Ryan

Bermúdez's first experience with the IIRP was at a Real Justice (an IIRP program) restorative practices training in the late 1990s, in Rochester, New York, with IIRP director of training Bob Costello. Bermúdez was impressed with the philosophy and methods she learned about in that presentation, and saw the potential implications for her own work, said Costello. Eventually she asked the IIRP to work with CASES.

Before Community Prep embarked on its second year, Bermúdez called on the IIRP to train the staff. Wrote Rimer, "The school reopened in Manhattan last fall with a new staff trained in an approach that had been successful at eight privately run schools for delinquent youth in Pennsylvania. It emphasized structure and high expectations as well as counseling and support." The "approach" mentioned in *The New York Times* is restorative practices; the "eight privately run schools" are operated by the Community Service Foundation (www.csfbuxmont.org), the IIRP's sister organization.

Rimer's *Times* article depicts restorative practices in action, in the following account of a restorative justice conference held after a student threatened a teacher: "Administrators sat down with [the student], his mother and [the teacher]. While they made it clear to [the student] that his behavior was unacceptable, they also told him that he was bright, and that they wanted him in school. Ms. Bermúdez went through a series of questions with [the student]: What were you thinking [at the time]? Who did you affect by your actions, and how? What do you need to do to make things right?" After a few months of being in an environment where such interactions are commonplace, this student's behavior had improved enough for him to return to his neighborhood high school. There are many such success stories at Community Prep.

Mark Ryan, Community Prep's principal, told the eForum he is thrilled with the way restorative practices has helped the school, saying, "Students who had exhibited difficult, negative behavior before the implementation of restorative practices thrived in an environment of firm limits combined with abundant support. ... Restorative practices helped Community Prep High School become a safe community, a place where students can make real, meaningful changes in their lives."

Bob Costello, IIRP director of training, said Community Prep is "an unbelievably bold undertaking — to put so many of the worst-behaved kids in one building and give them an opportunity to make changes." The first year, he said, they had struggles, but these were "part and parcel of any start-up." The school staff "had beliefs that matched restorative practices, but they needed practical, hands-on stuff. We gave them a framework, a common language and strategies that matched their philosophy."

Costello stressed that Community Prep's staff has had to figure out how to use what the IIRP has taught them. "They've done all the hard work, setting up their own schedules and organization," he said. He added that the staff has been "remarkably open to feedback" and has actively sought out the IIRP's guidance. "It takes guts to ask for help," he added.

Costello brought up another critical issue. "The question everyone always asks is: Will this work with New York City kids? Will this work with tough kids?" His answer: "These students are no different than students anywhere else. Their behavior is identical to kids' behavior anywhere. The differences are in intensity and frequency. Children are children."

The relationship between the IIRP and CASES is ongoing. Restorative practices has been so effective with the "tough New York City kids" at Community Prep that CASES plans to implement the approach in several other programs.

6

Restorative Practices
Impacts Minnesota Public Schools
....
An Interview with Nancy Riestenberg

Nancy Riestenberg is a prevention specialist with the Safe and Drug Free Schools program at the Minnesota (USA) Department of Education. She provides technical assistance and workshops on violence and bullying prevention, school connectedness, cultural relevance of prevention education and restorative measures. She was interviewed by Laura Mirsky at IIRP's Third International Conference on Conferencing, Circles and other Restorative Practices in August 2002.

BY LAURA MIRSKY
....

Q: How is restorative practices being implemented in public schools in Minnesota?

A: The whole range of restorative practices is happening in the schools: family group conferencing, restorative group conferencing, circles to repair harm, circles of understanding, victim offender dialogue. All of those practices are being tried to varying degrees in schools. The activity is at a relatively high level.

It's hard to keep track of it because people go to trainings and then they may do things that are difficult to see or to track. For instance, a teacher may go to a training and that may influence the way they conduct their classroom, or an administrator may go to a training and then handle discipline differently than what he or she did before. In some instances, school districts have taken a more holistic approach or a sort of institutional approach — they've actually changed some policy and decided to proactively train people. Activity is happening at all levels: at a kind of grassroots level, at a building level and in some instances at a district level.

Q: How has restorative practices changed the schools where they're being used?

> "With restorative practices, you create a safe place, people can express their feelings. It creates an environment where empathy can happen."
>
> — Nancy Riestenberg

A: It's hard to quantify that. I would say that it's changed the way people do their job and their attitudes toward their jobs. It's not uncommon for me to hear administrators say, "I like my job more," "I feel more confident that I'm really getting to the root of the problem," "I feel as though by doing this I make better connections between students and teachers," "I feel as though I have more connections with the students that I work with." The atmosphere in the building might feel better, more comfortable, more respectful. Others feel that their teaching has improved, that they're making connections with children, seeing children being empowered. It's always fun when a kid can ask for a talking piece and hold a circle in the corner of the playground with his friends and feel as though they have taken care of their problems themselves. When kids learn a problem-solving process and they practice it, it becomes their own; they figure out how they can do it themselves.

Q: What appeals to you about restorative practices?

A: I have always worked in the fields of prevention and education. I have dealt with social issues. One of the issues that intrigued me was bullying. There has always been a question in my mind about the school's response to this and how they might do it differently. If we suspend bullies or make them sit out from recess, how does that help them or make them change their behavior? How can you help people figure out another way of behaving so they don't hurt other people? I think a good restorative process attempts to get at that and gives people some ideas. It is also a place where people can begin to reflect on what they're doing and why they do it.

The other thing that appealed to me about restorative practices involves empathy. I spent a lot of time working in the area of child sexual abuse prevention education. One of the things that struck me is that one of the reasons why offenders do what they do — this most horrific act — is because they either don't know how to or have decided not to empathize with someone. If they were to stop for a moment and think about what this would be like, they just could not go down that road. I know that the skills of empathy can be taught. The parts of empathy can be taken apart, explored and looked at, but you can't make someone empathize with someone else. With restorative practices, you create a safe place, people are prepared, they're supported, they're there with their friends or their family and they know that they can express their feelings. Everybody is part of figuring out how to solve a problem. I think it creates an environment where empathy can happen. So you can lead them to the water and hope that they will drink in the process.

In terms of prevention, that is such a key element. If we can get people to be able to empathize with each other, they're so much less likely to hurt one another. It's a place where you can both teach it and hold out the possibility of people being able to actually practice it.

Q: You did a three-year evaluation of the restorative practices in your school districts. Could you tell us about it?

A: We had money from the legislature to evaluate the implementation and results of using restorative practices in four different school districts. We had an urban kindergarten through eighth grade building, a suburban school district with three buildings and a consolidated rural district that had three buildings and a rural high school. This was an evaluation. It was not research, so we didn't have control groups and all those sorts of things. This was really about gathering information, about telling the story of how they went about doing this and what kind of preliminary outcomes they saw. There were a number of things that emerged from this evaluation. I think one of the most important, and for some people reassuring, things that we found out is that to make change happen in a school you need to have at least two to three years. Just because somebody gets money in July, they're not going to be able to implement immediately in September and then start testing it in January. Nothing happens that fast in a school. That's a very important thing for people to remember if they are going to sustain any kind of energy in trying to create change in a building or among people. It takes time. Even with people who have the heart, soul, energy, resources and desire, it still takes time.

Another thing that we found is that it's easy to gather information about of-fenders, about what kind of an impact a restorative process might have had on them and whether or not they reoffended. It's a little bit harder to gather information about the impact on the person

Students pass the "talking piece."

who was hurt or on the community. It doesn't show up as numbers, so you don't have it on the discipline track. "We had five victims last month and this month we only have two" — nobody keeps numbers like that. How would you define them anyway? That's kind of hard. That has to be defined by the person. Therefore, you have to use other ways of figuring out how to evaluate. You have to ask people questions and you have to go with their per-ceptions and feelings. That gives you a richer piece of information, but it's more qualitative than quantitative. The other thing I think we learned from this it that you really need to put the two together. You have to have numbers and you have to have the stories. You need to have both of those things together to get a clear under-standing about what happened and to figure out what you can learn from that.

In one building in particular there were very strong quantitative results. It appears that with the institution of circles to repair harm, along with circles used in the classroom for building community, they went from about seven incidents of violence a day to around one a day in the course of three and a half years. That was a significant drop. There was also a significant drop over three years in terms of overall behavior referrals to the office. They went from somewhere in the thousands to 450 over the course of three years. That drop was an all-school effort. It was not the effort of just one person. It was the administrative team making decisions to do things differently, as well as quite a number of staff people deciding that they were going to include this community-building activity in their classroom.

That was another key thing we learned from the evaluation. If you just have a restorative intervention, that will get you someplace. If you just have classroom management skills that are cognitively based and are about problem solving rather than using power and control over kids, you will get someplace. If you get the two of them together, you will go so much farther in a quicker period of time because the whole school then becomes congruent. There are lots of classroom management approaches that are cognitively based. They're about problem solving. They're about helping individual children learn how to make amends, use conflict resolution, etc. That's been around for a long time and there's been good research on it indicating that it's very helpful, useful and that it makes the classroom a better place. But when you have the inevitable fight, which is going to happen no matter what, then what do you do? Are you going to be able to continue to carry the philosophy that you built up so nicely in the classroom into the principal's office, or are you going to have to go back to suspensions and expulsions? So restorative interventions help to complete a kind of circle of support, if you will, for children within the school. The message is: We recognize that people are going to make mistakes, but that doesn't mean that you have to leave the community. We have this other way to hold you accountable and help you fix the problem that you made. That was a very interesting observation — when you put the two together, you just got further faster.

Q: Do you have any particular stories that you would like to share?

A: There's one story that I like to tell about four third-grade boys: three African-American boys and one European-American boy. This was in a sub-

Boys make a connection during a circle.

urban district, so the African-American boys were very much in the minority; about 10 percent of that school were kids of color. The white boy called the other three boys a racial slur. In this district that was considered a bottom-line behavior, which meant it was racial harassment and he could have been suspended for probably two or three days.

The boys were familiar with the circle process and the administrators were willing to consider a restorative response to the offense. The boys all agreed that they wanted to sit in a circle and talk about what had happened. The restorative justice planner in that school facilitated the circle. The significant thing that came out of the circle was that the three African-American boys had an opportunity to tell the boy what that slur meant. For one boy, it was the word that a white man used when he shot his uncle in the head. The second boy said, "It's the word those men in the white sheets use in the movies when they go to burn down my people's houses." The third boy said when he hears that word, "It just hurts my heart so much I just have to leave; I have to get away." I think the offending boy knew it was a powerful word, but I kind of want to believe that in third grade he didn't know just how powerful it was. He does now. He certainly knows now.

> In one building they went from about seven incidents of violence a day to around one a day in the course of three and a half years.

I thought the boy received a gift from those other boys. They had the courage to share that with him. What they wanted from this kid, to make amends for what he had done, was for them to be friends. So for the rest of that year, they played together on the playground. Three years later, the woman who ran that group said that they still played together. They were still friends. That's one of my favorite stories.

In another school incident, a fight broke out among about four or five boys. This fight happened, of course, in a context. It happened a couple of weeks after a boy in that school died in a tragic car accident. One boy made some disparaging remarks about the deceased — that what happened was probably his fault. Maybe he wasn't wearing his seat belt, or he was driving too fast, or he was impaired in some way. He was blaming the person who had died, in a way. Some of the friends of the boy who had died heard this and were incensed. It was very recent. Grief was still very high in everybody's mind and they jumped him. They all got into a fight.

The boys would normally have been suspended for at least three days for a fight. But, in this particular instance, they all agreed to go to the restorative justice planner in the school. They wanted to have a circle to talk about what happened. As they talked about how their behavior had affected themselves and other people, they all came to the conclusion that the person they had harmed the most was the boy who had died. To make amends for this, they all got into the restorative justice planner's car and they went to the graveyard and apologized to the gravestone. It's that kind of creativity that is so compelling for me, where you can have a connection between the true harm and the consequence. That is profound. Not only is it profound, I'm sure that it was also therapeutic for these boys. I bet it was probably healing for them. I think that it helped them to appreciate more what they had lost. That's the kind of connection we need as human beings. That's what being a human being is about. It's not about the recipe of the student conduct book. Those are some of my favorite stories.

Q: What advice would you give someone who wants to bring restorative practices into their school?

A: I guess the first thing that I would advise people is that if they are in a position to do it and they believe in it, they should just do it. There's a lot of autonomy amongst the adults in a school, and wherever you can find it, even if it is just with the low-level stuff, it is a good way to operate. In doing that, you can do that grassroots kind of building where people hear about things and they become intrigued. They come because of their own interest to try to find out about something. If you are a person who does have a position of power, then maybe what you want to do is try to go at the top end. I think that you just need to decide what your sphere of influence is and start there.

Another piece of advice is part of the restorative philosophy: This is a process that should be voluntary. Just let go of the idea that everybody in a school is supposed to do this and that every incident needs to be handled this way and everybody needs to be a believer and everybody needs to participate. That's a road to exhaustion. Look for people who are friends. Look for people who are compatible. Look for people who would be advocates with you. Go where the strengths are. Do that in a respectful way. That's what the philosophy calls people to do.

I think the other thing that is important in trying to do something in a school is that if you get to a position where you can do training, involve kids in the training. It makes a big difference. It gives people a different per-

Sixth-grade students take part in a circle at Kaposia Elementary School, in South St. Paul, Minnesota.

spective on kids to see them in a different setting. They offer an enormous amount of wisdom and perspective.

Q: What do you see, hope, dream is the future of restorative practices in schools?

A: I hope that this is not a fad like a lot of other things. I'm concerned that people don't co-opt the term just to appease people, that they don't just call certain things restorative when they're not. I think a good example of that is community service. Community service is a wonderful thing. It can be an extraordinary way for kids to learn. It's a great way to teach people. It can be part of a restorative agreement where you use community service as a means to make amends. But when you tell somebody to do community service, just because it's community service doesn't mean it's restorative. You're missing those steps of coming together, talking about who was affected and then deciding together what would be some ways to repair this harm. If one of the things that they figure out is, "Oh, it would be cool if you did community service. You took time away from edu-cation, so why don't you tutor in the classroom? You're good at math." That's very different than saying, you took time away in the hallway, so now I want you to go to community service.

If you just have a restorative intervention, that will get you someplace. If you just have classroom management skills that are cognitively based and are about problem solving rather than using power and control over kids, you will get someplace. If you get the two of them together, you will go so much farther in a quicker period of time because the whole school then becomes congruent.

I hope I come to a point where I will be able to ask school people if they have policies attending to the needs of victims in their school and they will be able to answer yes. They will be able to articulate what those are. There will be things offered to kids when they have been harmed, harassed, bullied or part of a fight — the opportunity to talk to someone, to get education, to be able to ask for a restorative process. I would hope that we could come to a time when the school is not just focused on the person who did the harm, but is equally focused on the person who was harmed. Pairing punishment with restorative processes is perhaps problematic. People do it because it satisfies both sides. Certainly, even if you suspend the child, doing the restorative process pays attention to the victim, but I hope that we would get to a place where we would not have to do the two of them together, that people would be satisfied with restorative consequences.

> The message is: We recognize that people are going to make mistakes, but that doesn't mean that you have to leave the community. We have this other way to hold you accountable and help you fix the problem that you made.

I hope that people make the connection between restorative interventions and the way the staff is trained to talk to kids, to manage their classroom and to try to help the kids with their behavior. I would like to see them make the connection between restorative interventions and the health curriculum they teach about problem solving and decision making. I would hope for school people to have enough time somewhere in their lives where they can stop and breathe and see the larger picture.

7

Transforming
School Culture
....
A SaferSanerSchools Update

BY LAURA MIRSKY
....

The IIRP's SaferSanerSchools program has grown considerably since its initial pilot projects. The program is helping schools implement restorative practices, an approach that engages students to take responsibility for their behavior, thereby building school community and safety.

Restorative practices is being implemented in schools all over the world, as has been reported in *The New York Times, The Philadelphia Inquirer, MetroKids Pennsylvania* and *School Board News.*

Below are accounts of a few of the many schools using circles, "restorative questions" (What were you thinking about at the time? Who did you affect by your actions, and how? What do you need to do to make things right?) and other practices to build a restorative school culture. Administrators and teachers are developing lots of creative ways to implement the approach.

Holy Innocents Elementary School is one of five inner-city parochial elementary schools in Philadelphia, Pennsylvania, USA, implementing restorative practices with help from SaferSanerSchools.

Eighth-grade students take part in a circle at Holy Innocents Elementary School, Philadelphia.

The entire staff at Holy Innocents has been trained in restorative practices. Every teacher conducts at least one classroom circle a week, and most teachers feel that this has been very worthwhile, said the school's principal, Sister Shaun Thomas. Teachers are also using circles in faculty meetings. That has been "an incredible adventure," she said, "because a lot more has been said, and there's a lot more insights into people and where they're coming from than in the past."

Holy Innocents recently merged with three parish schools closed by the Archdiocese of Philadelphia. The school's multicultural student population (African-

American, Caucasian, Hispanic, Vietnamese) resides in several different neighborhoods. Restorative practices has definitely helped with that merger, said Sister Thomas.

Seniors "circle up" at Souderton Area High School in Pennsylvania.

Elizabeth McCollum, an eighth-grade teacher at the school, said that the approach has provided an open line of communication, allowing students to feel safe. With four schools from different parishes combining into one, gang activity increased, said McCollum. The restorative approach has helped students realize that there are other ways to resolve conflicts besides fighting. "Students told us about an incident with another student that they felt was unsafe for others," she said. "I don't think they would have felt safe telling us that before."

Circles build school community, said McCollum. She told a story about a boy in the school with cerebral palsy. In a circle held to discuss harassment and bullying, a student announced, "There's someone in the eighth grade who's being mistreated, who will not speak up for him or herself, and I won't tolerate it." Another student seconded that sentiment and apologized for mistreating others herself. "That was huge," said McCollum. "We experienced a great high of really incorporating this student into the community. They play football with him now out in the schoolyard."

Holy Innocents is utilizing restorative practices as part of a five-year Middle States Association of Colleges and Schools reaccreditation project. Asked how restorative practices fits with a Catholic school, Sister Thomas said she thought it fits with any educational institution: "In a school, teachers have a right to teach and children have a right to learn, and restorative practices is a way to address behavior that works against that."

The semirural Souderton Area School District, in Montgomery County, Pennsylvania, is implementing restorative practices in three secondary schools. Assistant high school principal Chris Hey said that they contacted SaferSanerSchools "to make a positive change." Although theirs is a stable community, he said, school spirit was low, and they were disciplining "the same kids over and over again."

An implementation team of teachers, guidance counselors and administrators from the three schools received restorative practices training. Now teachers and administrators are using circles and restorative discipline approaches. Staff get together to share stories about what's working and what's not.

Restorative practices is helping to build relationships and community in the classroom. "We've had some students who are really disengaged, who'd rather sleep through class," said Hey. Now, because students are given an opportunity in circles to speak every day, and because they know each other better, they're more engaged in the learning process. "I definitely see a change in those kids," said Hey. "They're not getting referred to us as much for behavior because they have a bigger stake in the classroom. Kids who last year had really combative relationships with us are now on our side and really trying to do better."

Reaction from parents to the restorative philosophy has been very positive, said Hey, adding, "Parents really appreciate that we're giving their kids a voice in the process and that kids are making amends for what they've done."

Perry Engard, a business teacher at Souderton High School, finds circles and restorative questions very helpful. (He even uses the questions at home with his three-year-old.) Engard often opens class with a circle, incorporating lesson content. For a class on employment contracts, he asked, "What was the most unreasonable — or — reasonable treatment you've witnessed by an employer with an employee?" This introduced the legal concept of reasonable treatment by an employer, while exploring restorative philosophy.

Initially, Engard resisted using restorative practices for discipline. Then he caught two students cheating on a homework assignment and decided to hold a circle. Without naming names, he described the incident, and then asked, "If you caught people cheating, how would you think it should be handled?" A girl said, "I can't stand it when people want to copy my homework." Hearing her, the wrongdoers took responsibility for their actions. There has been no cheating in class since.

Souderton High Spanish teacher Tammy Caccavo does check-in and check-out circles at the beginning and end of class periods, which has helped build community in her classes. The kids love the circles, she said, discussing their hopes and goals and such topics as responsibility and respect. Because of the circles, she said, there has been little need to discipline her classes. Caccavo held a circle on parents' night to demonstrate the process, which was very well received.

At Souderton's Indian Crest Junior High School, restorative circles with students, teachers, guidance counselors and facilitators are now used regularly, said assistant principal Joyce Kemmerling. Consequently, students are not repeating negative behaviors, and their relationships with teachers are stronger. Kemmerling said that she likes the idea of working with students, "so that they own, not only their behavior, but the repair work and the amends that need to be done as a result of their actions. I think that happens because they reflect on who it impacted."

Children love the restorative approach, she said, "but when they're asked a restorative question they say, 'That's a really hard question!' They're not used to being asked to reflect on their behavior. They're used to getting their consequences and leaving. And they come up with harder consequences for themselves than we would. That's important; it means that they see that their behavior is serious." Parents appreciate that their children are involved in the discipline process, said Kemmerling.

Indian Crest learning-support teacher Doug Henning (whose students have learning, emotional or behavioral issues) thinks that restorative practices can be as effective in learning support classes as they are in other classes. Since implementation began, he said, disciplinary referrals have decreased and student behavior has improved.

> "In a school, teachers have a right to teach and children have a right to learn, and restorative practices is a way to address behavior that works against that."
>
> — Sister Shaun Thomas

Henning thinks it's important to introduce restorative practices such as circles as opportunities to share and get to know each other, rather than as punishment. He has regular check-in and check-out circles. Monday is "good and new day," when students share one good or new thing. Friday is "smiles and cries day," when they share something happy or sad. Henning thinks these circles enhance the classroom environment, and because kids enjoy the process, it can be used to address behavior and conflicts.

When Henning missed class one day, his students treated the substitute teacher very poorly. The next day, he held a circle with the class and the substitute. She told the students that their behavior had upset her; he shared his embarrassment and disappointment. The students, surprised, were contrite and eager to repair the harm. They followed through with personal apologies and letters. The next time Henning was out, the students treated the substitute teacher much better.

Stoddart-Fleisher Middle School, in inner-city Philadelphia, serves students from low-income, government-subsidized housing and the neighboring community, including area homeless shelters. Once cited as a "failing school," Stoddart-Fleisher is among the Philadelphia schools that are run by Edison Schools, a private-sector school-management company. Stoddart-Fleisher subsequently achieved "Adequate Yearly Progress," as mandated by the U.S. No Child Left Behind Act, said principal Tom Davidson. But, he said, "Kids' behavior wasn't improving. The suspension rate was embarrassingly high." He asked SaferSanerSchools to train the staff in restorative practices, and they're in the beginning stages of implementation.

The staff found the SaferSanerSchools training "realistic, not theoretical," said Davidson, adding "[the trainers] didn't come in and say, 'What you're doing is wrong; what we suggest is right.' We were treated as professionals, not looked down upon, which is often the feeling staff has about outside consultants."

The staff is intrigued with what they've learned and are experimenting with the restorative principles, including the restorative questions. "When kids act up we have them write out the answers to the questions. They're engaged in thinking about their actions. Then they talk to the teacher and any victim that was involved," said Davidson.

Davidson sees the approach as a perfect fit for the school. "Everything we should be doing in a school is about teaching, whether it's imparting subject matter or about how human beings should relate to one another and how to resolve conflicts. Restorative practices gives us a better framework to teach about those situations." He concluded, "Restorative practices is a phenomenon that's beginning to take hold in Philadelphia."

8

Restorative Practices
at Queanbeyan South
An Australian Primary School

BY ABBEY J. PORTER

Restorative practices has proved a success at a primary school in Australia, where teachers have discovered that discipline works much better when the children themselves take part in the process.

A few years ago, Queanbeyan South Public School, in New South Wales, just outside the Australian capital of Canberra, was struggling with persistent problems of bullying, violence and truancy among its pupils. Conventional punishments like detentions and suspensions didn't seem to help. "We were just chasing our tails," recalled teacher Elizabeth Harley, who said that disrespect for authority and low self-esteem were common among the students.

The school has an ethnically diverse student body of about 660 children, many from low-income households. Aboriginal children, who make up about 15 percent of the student population, presented a particular challenge, Harley said, in part because many had parents who, often due to their own negative school experiences, did not support their children's schooling.

Said Harley, "Our suspension records were the highest in Queanbeyan, and we had a number of kids in detention on a regular basis." But, she realized, placing children in detention wasn't doing them any good. "They began to treat it as a bit of a joke. For the hard-core, repeat offenders, it wasn't making any difference whatsoever."

"Once children got into this antisocial behavior and were punished at school, it usually lent itself to further

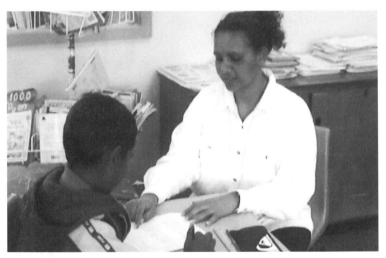

A student and teacher work together at Queanbeyan South Primary School.

alienation," said principal Paul Britton, a veteran educator. Separating children from school isolates them from their peers, causes them to miss schoolwork and gives them more opportunities to develop problem behaviors, he pointed out.

Ready to try a different approach, Britton contacted Matt Casey, a former police officer who trains schools and social service providers in restorative practices through Real Justice Australia, an affiliate of the International Institute for Restorative Practices. In January 2003, Casey conducted a training session for teachers and administrators at Queanbeyan South. He introduced a restorative approach to discipline that encourages students to talk about and reflect on their behavior, take responsibility for their actions and find ways to "make things right" with those they have hurt.

Britton liked the idea that "children were forced to face the consequences of their actions, meet face-to-face with their victims and do something to make things better." The approach also seemed an excellent fit with the culture of caring, support and respect that Britton was promoting in the school.

Casey encouraged teachers to think about the relationships they developed with their pupils, advocating a "firm but fair" approach, with a high level of control and discipline but also plenty of support and encouragement. He also introduced staff to the "script" at the heart of the restorative approach: a list of questions that asks victim and offender to reflect on the incident in question and come up with appropriate ways to make amends. The questions, which include: Who has been affected by what you have done? and What impact has this incident had on you and others? — can be used in a variety of situations, from informal interventions in playground disputes to formal conferences in which the affected parties address the transgression.

The questions reflect a non-blaming approach, said Britton. The first one, What happened?, is far less accusatory than What did you do? Said Britton, "With the script, kids know someone will listen to their side of things." Knowing that their side has been heard, they are far more likely to accept the agreed-upon consequences.

Britton emphasizes the fact that the restorative approach gives children an opportunity to repair the harm

A Queanbeyan South Primary School pupil shows off her sunny attitude.

they have caused. He has found that the last question on the script, What do you think you need to do to make things right?, is key to that process: "Often, that will build a bridge between the victim and the perpetrator."

Britton saw that happen in one case in which children sold fake raffle tickets to senior citizens. After a conference was held, the offenders paid back the money and performed gardening for an elderly victim as restitution. This restored the relationship between the children and the woman they had wronged, who came to see them as "young boys, instead of hoodlums."

For teachers like Elizabeth Harley, the restorative approach was not dramatically different from business as usual — talking things out, developing relationships and trying to understand where the children were coming from. But Harley believes that Casey's training provided such methods with more credibility among the more authoritarian, punitive teachers, who thought that talking things out was "too soft" or a "cop-out." "It changed their approach with children," said Harley. "Quite a number of them found that they had results, and it was a lot easier to talk things through."

> "Little kids are good at knowing what to do to make things right. It's a matter of being able to ask the right questions."
>
> — Elizabeth Harley

The program also provided structure and consistency. "When we decided as a school that we would all follow this program, that was the thing that turned the school around," said Harley. "Every teacher started a very organized and structured approach. When conflicts occurred, we followed the Real Justice script, and the children knew that script."

The children proved to be surprisingly good self-disciplinarians, ready to negotiate with each other and take responsibility for their behavior. "A lot of them are prepared to say, 'I've done something wrong, and I'll accept the consequences,'" said Harley. "Little kids are good at [knowing] what to do to make things right. It's a matter of being able to ask the right questions."

Restorative practices has brought about many changes at Queanbeyan South. In the two years since Matt Casey conducted his initial training session, the incidence of student violence, detentions and suspensions has plunged dramatically. The school's "detention room" has become a "conference room." The prospect of going through the conference script has proved an effective deterrent. "Some of the students hated having to answer those questions," Harley chuckled, "and that alone stopped many of them from going into detention."

While the approach has produced positive effects throughout the school, the results have been "especially spectacular" among Aboriginal students, said Britton. In 2004, not one Aboriginal child was suspended at Queanbeyan South, a school whose indigenous population once had a reputation for violence and gang activity.

Above all, restorative practices has brought about a positive change in the culture of the school. "We've got the best morale we've ever had," said Britton. "People feel good about themselves, and the children seem to be happier. They feel more enfranchised, and that people care about them. I believe Real Justice is a part of all that."

Britton also believes there is now more learning going on in the school. "Children try harder because they know they're not going to be condemned for failure or mistakes," he said. With restorative practices, problematic behaviors are censured while the worth of the individual is upheld. "We always focus on the thing that has gone wrong, rather than the person," Harley explained. "I think it's had a general raising of self-esteem with a lot of these children, who suddenly believe, 'I can talk my problems out.'"

Parents, too, are more supportive and less resentful of restorative methods than of the usual disciplinary measures. Restorative practices encourages family involvement, and parents appreciate the opportunity to participate. Britton recalled one case in which two children had assaulted another child, and the parents of the victim and perpetrators took part in a conference to hash out consequences. "The parents were part of the solution, rather than just being on the receiving end," he said.

Parental involvement also helps ensure that children's promises of restoration are kept. Restorative practices works especially well with the indigenous community, said Britton, as the sense of kinship is strong among them, and members of the extended family tend to get involved in their children's disciplinary issues.

Trainer Matt Casey encourages teachers to look for ways to use restorative practices "in every instance with kids, rather than waiting for things to go wrong." He believes that restorative practices can lead students and teachers to a better understanding of themselves and of others. "It starts you on a path where you find you must reevaluate your behavior on every level," said Casey. "You can't just leave it at the school door and walk out."

Britton, too, thinks that restorative practices could have far-reaching effects. By reducing animosity and breaking down barriers between students and groups, he believes, restorative practices is preparing the children of Queanbeyan South to deal with issues far beyond the classroom. "They might go out and help make the world a little bit better, rather than worse," said Britton. "If we build bridges instead of walls, we've got a far better chance."

9

A New Reality
for Troubled Youth in Hungary

BY LAURA MIRSKY

A two-year demonstration project, Community Service Foundation (CSF) Hungary, began in Budapest in January 2003 — its goal· to implement restorative practices with delinquent and at-risk youth. The school was funded by grants from CSF and the International Institute for Restorative Practices (IIRP) in the United States and the Hungarian Ministry of Children, Youth and Sports.

The Hungarian ministries of Justice and of Social and Family Affairs supported the school as "a model for institutions to work with children with problems or at risk," said Vidia Negrea, the school's director.

The CSF school was an important turning point for Hungary. As a matter of course, delinquent youth in that country are removed from their home environment and housed in reformatories or other special institutions, put on probation or jailed. Negrea explained: "There is essentially no law in Hungary supporting day treatment." She hoped that the school would give troubled youth a better chance to reintegrate into society by providing an alternative approach in their own community. A new law took effect in June 2003 acknowledging the need for services provided by NGOs (nongovernmental organizations), in effect encouraging entities like CSF Hungary.

Working as a psychologist at the largest, oldest boys' reformatory in Europe, in Aszod, Hungary, Negrea saw that the methods in use there weren't working. Research data on 500 boys showed that six months after leaving the reformatory, 75 percent had reoffended. Data analysis revealed that the boys who had most closely followed reformatory rules had reoffended sooner and more often than others.

Boys at the reformatory told Negrea that they were scared to go home, afraid of being labeled for life as "bad" and terrified of meeting the victims of their crimes and their families. To address this fear, she asked 100 students in her care to write an imaginary letter to their victims. Their heartfelt, remorseful letters had Negrea and her colleagues in tears. Some boys sent the letters to their victims, apologizing for the harm they had done to them and their families and offering any help they might provide. This was the first time Negrea felt she came close to fulfilling people's needs, both victims and offenders, instead of just administering punishment.

Negrea received her first training in restorative practices when Beth Rodman and Paul McCold of the IIRP came to Hungary. She was thrilled to finally find a framework for dealing with troubled youth similar to her experience with the letter-writing project at the reformatory. She later spent a year doing hands-on training in restorative practices at CSF schools in Pennsylvania and was determined to bring the fruits of her training back to Eastern Europe.

She also appreciated the restorative work environment created for the staff, where mutual support was a workplace priority. Said Negrea: "My friends and colleagues at home deserve a place where they are happy to come to work, even with the most difficult students. Here at CSF, I realized it was possible."

> "In Hungary, like every other country that was under the socialists for so many years, somebody always decided *FOR* you what you had to do, or told you what *TO* do." For that reason, Negrea thinks, the notion of doing things *WITH* people will be especially beneficial for Hungary.

At first, Negrea wasn't confident that she could lead such an effort. Near the end of her stay in the United States, IIRP president Ted Wachtel suggested that Negrea try being a supervisor. When she served as a substitute supervisor at two CSF schools, she gained confidence working in new settings. "It was a great opportunity to see what I had learned and how my learning would apply elsewhere," she noted.

The key to the work, Negrea discovered, "was not about being knowledgeable about everything happening in each particular school and having all the answers, but about using the same way of working with people and being responsible and respectful with people. The structure and philosophy were the same." Negrea realized that her work in Hungary would be based on implementing the same structure and philosophy.

When she went home to Hungary in 2001, Negrea quit her two jobs: as a psychologist at the boys' reformatory and at the National Institute for Family and Children, and began to try to introduce restorative practices. Some of Negrea's colleagues told her that Hungary wasn't ready for those methods. "It's not America," they said. But Negrea understood that restorative practices were "not based on American culture, but on relationships between people."

Negrea drew on her existing relationships with people in social services — students, probation officers, teachers, administrators, police — and "made a lot of noise" about why restorative practices is important. She was then asked to do trainings for government institutions that wanted to make changes. "I used to be sent in as an expert to say why things weren't going well," said Negrea, adding, "They expected me to report on how to change or close the institutions."

Instead, Negrea did two-day Introduction to Restorative Practices trainings with all the employees at several institutions, "not just teachers and counselors, but the gatekeeper, the cook, the director." Negrea told them: "If you really want to change, you have to think about how you can work together, otherwise, they're going to close you down."

Negrea was struck by how quickly people understood the practices she introduced. "Very simple people can understand in hours that it's their responsibility to change the institution," she said. The institutions stayed open and are now using restorative circles. In one big group home, a semi-secure unit "where children are sent because nobody else can deal with them," the staff is using circles for themselves and with the children. At first it was strange for the staff to discuss their problems with each other. They were accustomed to blaming each other and relying on a hierarchy. But now they are expressing their issues openly and the children are developing their own group "norms" — standards for behavior.

Negrea also did restorative practices presentations for prosecutors, judges, lawyers, probation officers, school-teachers and administrators — people who would refer children to her CSF school. She used IIRP training videos and overhead projections, which had been translated into Hungarian, as well as interactive exercises.

To elucidate the social discipline window (Figure 1), which illustrates the concepts of TO, FOR, NOT, and WITH, she tried an exercise at one of her presentations that was originally developed in a CSF Professional Learning Group. Dividing the participants into four groups, she gave each group the same simple task to perform (drawing a flower). She then did NOT do anything and completely neglected one group (little support or control); did the entire task FOR another (high support, little control); dictated TO another group exactly what to do (high control, little support); and gave the WITH group the help they needed, but let them perform the task themselves.

By the end of the exercise, the participants had obtained a thorough, visceral understanding of the restorative paradigm. People in the neglected group felt hurt because they were being ignored. Those in the FOR group sat there and did nothing, upset that they had no input. The TO group members were angry and resentful at being told what to do. The people in the WITH group were happy and productive, having been treated restoratively: that is, with both high support and high control.

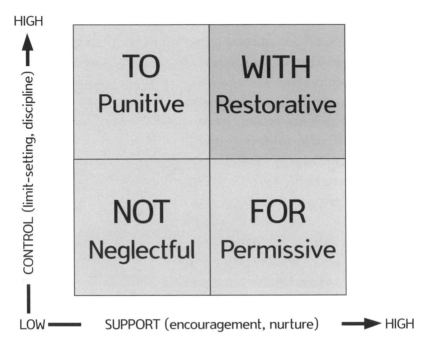

Figure 1. The Social Discipline Window.

In all, the restorative practices presentations went extremely well. "I was amazed," said Negrea, adding, "Nobody wanted to break for lunch; they wanted to keep going." Instruction in Hungary is traditionally very intellectual and theoretical, said Negrea. The restorative practices trainings, in contrast, were dynamic and interactive, based on real practice and understanding through action and reflection.

The trainings were a revelation. One teacher said that, deep inside, she had always known about the concepts Negrea had shared, but had never had the words for them, never known how simple and obvious they could be. Said Negrea, "I wanted the authorities to realize that they needed the program."

Negrea's strategy worked. At a presentation for police, some of them realized that they had been talking on the phone about the same students for a long time without ever meeting each other. They talked about their need to start working with each other and not just in a formal way. "Like a small but good virus, it spread," said Negrea. The idea was to disseminate restorative practices everywhere. "Children at the school took what they learned home with them and it affected their families," said Negrea.

CSF Hungary director Vidia Negrea (far right), poses with students and staff.

The pilot school began with four students, ages 13 to 16, all children at risk who were expelled from school: two who had used drugs, one with a criminal record and one with truancy problems. Students were referred to the school from group homes all over Budapest.

The school worked with 58 students over the two-year period. All did very well at CSF Hungary. These were kids who never wanted to come to school, but at CSF they came on time every day, even during heavy snowstorms. They helped each other get up in the morning by calling each other on the phone. "It was a tough group," said

Negrea, but she felt that the kids and the staff made great progress together.

"We did exactly the same things we did at the CSF school in Pennsylvania," said Negrea. "The same schedule, the same group structure, the same questions, the same 'feelings poster.'" And it all worked. Kids confronted each other and took responsibility for themselves and each other. "I thought it would be more difficult," said Negrea. But, she said, "the tough kids felt respected, so they had no reason to be disrespectful to the staff or to each other."

Feedback from parents was extremely positive. Negrea delighted parents by inviting them to attend intake interviews, along with the students and caseworkers. One parent exclaimed: "You mean we are going to be in the same room with our children and their social workers?" Said Negrea, "From the beginning, they have seen restorative practices and have been part of the program. Everybody had the chance to speak up." It was also a new thing for parents to be called with positive news from their children's school, a "good surprise" for them, said Negrea. One mother said that she never thought that her boy would go to school — that he never went before without being pushed.

Feedback from caseworkers was positive as well. Most caseworkers didn't believe students would come to the program. But, said Negrea, "every day we were viewed more and more seriously."

Negrea is hopeful that restorative practices will be good for Hungary. "Like every other country that was under the socialists for so many years," she said, "somebody always decided FOR you what you had to do, or told you what TO do." For that reason, she thinks, the notion of doing things WITH people will be especially beneficial for Hungary. (Socialism is not a bad thing in and of itself, Negrea believes, but it became an unsound system because people abused power.) "Restorative practices will be a good tool to help people develop fair relationships between people," she said. "Hungary needs that," she said, "and not just Hungary!"

A "feedback group," shown here, is a structured opportunity for community members to tell one another how their behavior affects them.

The effect of the CSF Hungary day treatment school pilot was quite significant, as the restorative concepts employed in the school have been implemented by children and youth agencies, alternative schools and reformatories throughout the country.

Zöld Kakas Líceum (Green Rooster alternative high school) is employing the entire continuum of restorative practices, from the informal to the formal, directly influenced by the experience of CSF Hungary. (Mária Kerényi, director of Zöld Kakas Líceum, presented a speech about the school at the IIRP's 10th World Conference, in Budapest, in November 2007.) "Green Rooster is very influential now in Hungary, as many education and social work students visit to learn about restorative practices," said Negrea.

In 2008, Negrea is teaching courses in restorative practices at two Hungarian universities, providing numerous trainings and working on several restorative practices projects with the Hungarian Ministry of Justice. She remains hopeful about the future of restorative practices in education and other fields in Hungary.

10

Report from Singapore
A High School Adopts Restorative Practices

BY JOSHUA WACHTEL

In 2005, Ping Yi Secondary School in Singapore was chosen by the Ministry of Education as one of four pilot schools to receive training and begin using restorative practices (RP). The school is now entering its fourth year of the pilot and is working to train teachers and administrators to use RP reactively in cases of discipline, but also proactively to create a restorative school culture.

Singapore is a prosperous industrial nation and center of trade for south Asia. The city sports beautiful high-rise office buildings as well as successful factories. The small island country about the size of Chicago (one of the few city-states in the modern world) has a population of over four million and sits just off the coast of Malaysia a few short miles north of the equator. The population is comprised of about 75 percent Chinese, 14 percent Malays, 9 percent Indians, and the rest Eurasians and other groups.

Ping Yi Secondary School (www.pyss.edu.sg), with 1,300 students ages 13 to 18, is located in a mature Singapore neighborhood (Chai Chee) with a population of about 90,000, on the eastern part of the island. The public school serves students from blue- and white-collar families alike.

In a society with a tradition of punitive discipline measures — including "caning," corporal punishment involving hitting a student with a rattan cane for the most serious offenses — RP is seen as a route to a more cooperative form of discipline and as a means to building better relationships between students and staff.

Said Julia Woo, principal of Ping Yi, "When Ping Yi embarked on the RP journey in 2005, we were looking for a disciplinary tool that could really work for our socially disadvantaged and disengaged students. Initially, the buy-in was slow as teachers were trying to reconcile the nonpunitive approach of RP to traditional punitive approaches." She added, "However, as we progressed in our RP journey and gained deeper understanding and insights into RP, the school began to see RP differently. It is not about discipline per se, but a whole-school philosophy that would trigger off curriculum reform, organizational change and re-culturation of the school."

Added Martin Chan, head of the department of pupil management at Ping Yi, "We were mindful at the beginning to package RP as something that teachers could and would want to use." A trainer from Australia delivered the initial three-day training, where teachers learned the restorative questions, the rationale behind RP and how it could help to correct behavior and build positive relationships. The restorative questions include: "What happened?" "Who was affected?" and "How do you and others feel about the incident?" These questions help children think about the impact of their actions. Added Chan, "We started with these generic questions and told our teachers, 'Maybe you're already doing these things, but we want to look at it from another perspective.'"

Chan said that shortly after the initial training he helped run a restorative conference for a senior class (4th year) where all the teachers found the group difficult to teach because students were constantly noisy and disruptive and seemed uninterested. First, teachers were asked if they would like to have a meeting with the students where they could tell them how they were being affected by their behavior. They agreed. The children were told about the idea, and they also seemed disposed to the meeting.

In a society with a tradition of punitive discipline measures — including "caning," corporal punishment involving hitting a student with a rattan cane for the most serious offenses — restorative practices is seen as a route to a more cooperative form of discipline and as a means to building better relationships between students and staff.

The students and teachers were arranged in a circle and the conference was held. During the conference, one teacher broke down and talked about how much she wanted to teach the class and how it hurt her because she couldn't. One student talked about how she was angry at the teachers because they were spending so much time scolding the misbehaving students, so she lost out on time for learning. One of the teachers apologized, saying, "I didn't see it from your point of view, but now I do." There were four students who were the most disruptive. It was clear that they were listening throughout the conference, and one spoke, apologizing to the teachers and the class.

Ping Yi Secondary School students participate in a restorative circle.

At the end of the conference, an agreement was reached where students who had been disruptive or had neglected to bring assignments to school would remove their desks to the hallway. A student came up with the idea and the teachers and class were all agreeable. They wrote the terms on a piece of paper and pinned it up in the classroom. Chan said that when he was making his rounds a few days later he saw four or five students with their desks out in the hallway. They were all craning their necks to try and see what was going on in the classroom. "It was amazing," said Chan. "Learning and teaching could again take place, and a couple months later all the students graduated."

Part of the discipline policy at the school is to give teachers independence and authority in their classes. "Teachers used to refer the slightest offenses to the discipline committee," said Chan. "It doesn't help if the administration comes in, and then the students think the teacher can't handle anything. RP provides a first round of intervention."

Part of the difficulty is making this work. When teachers started using the restorative questions the students began to say, "Why are all you teachers asking us the same questions?" Said Evelyn Choo, a social studies teacher at Ping Yi, "The students begin to give the answers they think we want to hear." She also said that for every 10 interventions it seems only one or two lead to positive changes in behavior.

But Choo has also had some very good experiences using RP. She oversees discipline for the second and third year students (equivalent to 10th and 11th grades in the U.S.) and she gets to meet a lot of parents. In one case where a student was frequently truant from school, she engaged the parents by holding a conference with them and their son. She started a restorative dialogue by asking the student, "Who has been affected by your truancy?" Having the parents present helped the student take a serious look at his actions.

"It's important to get the right people in," said Choo. For example, she's found that in cases of bullying it's really useful to bring the offender and the victim together. "The offender has to sit there and listen to the feelings of the victim," she said. "It really hits them to hear how the person feels, because they often just bully without thinking about it."

The idea to begin implementing RP in public schools in Singapore came after implementation of restorative justice (RJ) in the juvenile court system, starting about five years ago. (It could be said that this progression in Singapore echoes the development of RP in general, in that the principles of RJ have been adapted for use in other contexts, such as schools, social work and the workplace.) The Ministry of Education has since expanded its pilot to include more than 20 schools.

After the initial year of the pilot, a group of teachers and administrators went to Australia to witness firsthand the use of RP in several schools. According to Chan this gave the group "a total change of perspective. It gave a lot of hope to see it working in all the schools — from private schools to neighborhood schools." The group shared their experience with their fellow teachers when they returned and set a five-year target to become a restorative school by the year 2010.

The success of RP in a school is generally easiest to determine by qualitative measures. The positive feelings and atmosphere that pervades a school culture is what the team that visited Australia experienced so strongly. Still, there are quantitative measures that can be made. Chan and his colleague Ismail Bin Yusoff presented a report at the IIRP's 10th World Conference, in Budapest, Hungary, in November 2007, which showed that their implementation of RP correlated with reductions in the number of students who were late to school, the number of smoking offenses and the number of fights. Overall, from 2005 to 2007, the total number of disciplinary referrals dropped sharply from 500 to less than 200 per year (See "Toward a Restorative School," pp. 12-16, www.iirp.org/hu07/hu07_martin_yusoff.pdf).

This year Ping Yi will officially introduce the ideas of RP to student leaders. In the following year, the school hopes to formally educate parents about RP. The school leadership also supports an annual RP seminar for all the staff to take stock of what has happened and how to move forward with RP.

According to Chan, at the annual RP seminar there is a platform for sharing success stories and the hope is that these stories will rub off on others. "All the teachers are very caring; it's a very caring culture and the students know it," Chan concluded. "The bottom line now is about developing positive relationships with teachers, students and parents—all the stakeholders."

Woo believes that RP is helping to improve "the quality of relationships between all members of the school community." She said, "There is better communication and engagement of pupils as they feel that their voices are heard. My vision is to make RP a permanent feature of the school where RP is embedded in every aspect of school life, such as building a supportive school culture, a conducive learning environment and even in staff management." Woo concluded, "I hope that Ping Yi will be a success story for other schools and organizations to emulate in developing a professional working environment that is underpinned by restorative philosophy and practice."

11

Restorative Practices
and Organizational Change

The Bessels Leigh School

BY JOHN BOULTON, WITH LAURA MIRSKY

The Bessels Leigh School, in Abingdon, Oxfordshire, England, a residential special school for boys with emotional and behavioral difficulties, ages 11 to 16, has seen a remarkable change in culture, due to restorative practices.

Via restorative processes both formal and informal, the approximately 28 pupils are encouraged to express their emotions and feelings and consider those of others. In a very powerful way they are made aware of the consequences of their behavior and can recognize the harm that their actions have caused. In partnership with the IIRP and IIRP UK, Bessels Leigh School is on track to become a demonstration school for restorative practices in the UK.

Established in 1964, Bessels Leigh School formerly served mostly pupils at the milder end of the behavioral spectrum. The philosophy was traditional, structured and authoritarian. Pupils and staff were generally happy, boundaries were not severely tested, pupil-staff relationships were mostly positive and staff turnover was low.

About 12 years ago the client group began to change, due to the national political agenda, local government finances and a move to place the majority of youth in mainstream education.

Our disciplinary system, which had served well for so long, failed to meet the new challenges and actually contributed to the increasing problems.

We formerly used detentions at lunchtime or after school to punish minor behavioral infractions, a practice that was well-embedded and accepted. But some of the new, more difficult clientele challenged this. Staff were determined to carry out the punishment and physical confrontations ensued.

The sense of community was eroding. Staff-pupil relationships changed to an "us and them" situation, and vandalism and antisocial behavior increased dramatically. Staff suffered rising levels of stress, and absenteeism and turnover increased. There had to be a better, more harmonious way of working.

In 2004, I was invited to attend a course run by the Restorative Practices Training Association (an association between Thames Valley Police and IIRP UK) to become a restorative justice conference facilitator. The training provided a structure for many tenets that I feel should be central to all schools but are particularly necessary in the EBD (emotional and behavioral difficulty) sector.

After I delivered a day's training to familiarize our staff with restorative principles, we slowly began introducing them in the school. We cherry-picked cases for restorative conferences — those that more or less guaranteed success, or "no alternative" cases. We initiated practical projects involving the boys (such as planting a garden), so people could see the benefits.

Everything went well. A few staff came on board, but I didn't know how to initiate a more comprehensive process that would include more and more staff.

In September 2005, Nicola Preston (of IIRP UK) delivered the Introduction to Restorative Practices training to the school and residential unit staff. We were then able to put the theory into a practical context in terms of what we had achieved and what we wanted to do.

But the real turning point came when Nicola delivered the Using Circles Effectively training. Ever since I'd visited the Community Service Foundation and Buxmont Academy schools in America (demonstration programs of the IIRP) and had seen circles, I'd been tempted to use them at Bessels Leigh, but I was afraid they wouldn't work here, so I'd put it off. But after the circles training, the staff said, "We want to do this now."

> Restorative justice brought about change in the school as a reactive way of operating. Restorative practices empowered staff to take control of situations, raise issues, question behavior and examine their relationships with the boys and with each other.

The next day we held our first circle meeting with the boys. We soon instituted circle meetings at the end of every school day.

In these circles, we ask questions about the last 24 hours. A boy chairs the circle, and everyone has a chance to speak. "What has gone well?" brings out the positives. "What has not gone so well?" is followed by

"What have you done to put right the harm?" "What are you doing this evening?" ends the circle on a positive note.

The boys, with staff's help, established "norms," rules for running circles and for acceptable and safe behavior. Since the boys set the norms — not interrupting, not fidgeting, paying attention, etc. — they're more likely to respect them. New boys learn the norms from experienced boys; they're also posted on the walls. The norms have served the school well and, with prompting, are being adhered to.

Bessels Leigh students participate in a circle meeting.

At first the boys were sensitive and didn't like anybody, including their peers, bringing up issues, but they've become more accepting. We considered it a real milestone when the boys started passing comment about others, lending support and offering advice and help.

Another milestone occurred when a new boy enrolled in mid-year (as often happens). At his first circle meeting, before we got around to him, we made sure he saw how other boys were contributing, and to my amazement he just slotted right in. You could see him thinking, "Oh, it's going to be my turn shortly." We've since taken on several new boys, and they've also slotted right in. I attribute this to a change in our culture — "the way we do things here."

The boys have made the circle process their own. One day a staff member's camera went missing. We tried the usual methods to get information — nothing. Then a boy said to me, "I think we need a circle." Previous circles had involved eight or nine boys in the residential units. A whole-school circle meant getting all 28 boys together in one place, which I thought might be too difficult to handle. But the boy thought it was a good idea, and he offered to chair it.

All the boys gathered in the front hall. The boy facilitated the circle in a very mature way. Every boy contributed responsibly. There was no silliness. It was a real eye-opener for some staff who thought that these processes might not work for our school. Later that day, the camera was miraculously found in a bush.

Circles are embedded in our culture. In January 2006 we changed the school timetable to hold classroom circles each morning in addition to the unit-based evening circles. We've changed the staff schedule so they hold circles at least every fortnight. We've trained the domestic and secretarial staff in restorative practices, as some were still being abrasive with the boys. Now they're joining the circles.

Besides reintroducing a sense of community, restorative processes have greatly reduced property damage. We used to have a serious problem with boys breaking windows; one week we spent over £1,000 on windows. It had become the norm — get angry, break a window. Restorative practices virtually put an end to this.

For misdemeanors such as damage, boys and staff are involved in the restorative justice process, to attempt to repair harm done to the community. To make amends, boys have undertaken projects that benefit the whole school, including an "RJ Garden," a formal barbecue area (which helped end a problem with ad hoc fire setting) and a go-kart track.

Detentions have been replaced by catch-up sessions. When misbehavior disrupts a classroom, staff explain what they want to achieve in lessons, why attendance is important for everyone, and how catch-up sessions help make up for lost time. Now some boys attend catch-up sessions voluntarily, not because of misbehavior — perhaps they went to the dentist or whatever — but to get back on track.

The following two stories illustrate how culture change can happen:

A staff member was uneasy moving from the punitive (detention) system to the restorative (repairing harm). But when he became involved in the restorative justice process and worked with pupils to build a barbecue area, he realized that detention could never affect students in such a positive way.

Ten pupils worked on the RJ Garden project, yet only six were involved because of the restorative justice process; four were volunteers. Staff asked, "Is it punishment if others join in?" I answered, "Does it matter if the others are being positively engaged?"

I realized then that we were moving from a program of restorative justice to an ethos of restorative practices. Restorative justice brought about change in the school as a reactive way of operating. Restorative practices empowered staff to take control of situations, raise issues, question behavior and examine their relationships with the boys and with each other.

Three-Week Period	Negative Incidents	Negative Physical Incidents	Incidents of Damage
First 3 weeks of September '04	219	12	17
Last 3 weeks of Summer Term '05	362	13	10
First 3 weeks of September '05	164	9	3

Table 1. First term data, recording all significant incidents, comparing three three-week periods. The first three weeks of September 2005 immediately followed the restorative practices training by SaferSaner-Schools and the introduction of circle meetings.

Parents are also becoming involved in restorative processes; they're attending restorative conferences and have been pleased with the process and its outcomes. It's clear that boys are discussing the practices at home, as parents are asking us "What are these norms?" or "RP? What's that about?" This spring we plan to offer restorative training for parents.

The evidence strongly suggests that restorative practices has had a very real, positive impact on our school. The change is clear to the staff and to the boys, and our journey has just begun.

12

PEASE
Academy

The Restorative Recovery School

BY NANCY RIESTENBERG

PEASE Academy ("Peers Enjoying A Sober Education"), located in a church in Minneapolis, Minnesota, was the first recovery high school in the United States, founded in February 1989. In a recovery school, the students commit to working on recovery from chemical dependency and addiction while becoming successful students. Since all of the students attending the school have been in chemical dependency treatment, the safety of the environment is the first concern of students, their families and staff. Applying restorative principles and the process of the circle has helped this recovery school create a truly respectful, student-centered program.

During the last several years, through staff training and application, the school has incorporated the circle process and restorative principles into its program. Circles are used on Mondays and Fridays for youth to check in about the highs and lows in their sobriety. All 65 students and about five staff participate in the circles.

Circles are also used during the week as part of in-depth learning and community building. Sometimes students take turns being the circle facilitator or "keeper" and pose questions for the rest of the group of about 12. The language arts teachers use the circle in their writing classes, and some other teachers pass the talking piece to find out what students know, for instance, about the War of 1812. Using the talking piece ensures that each student will have the opportunity to participate.

But it is the circle for the student who has recently struggled with chemical use that has transformed the school the most. At PEASE, if a student uses drugs or alcohol and immediately asks for help, the student is able to remain at the school. They must be willing to learn from the experience and improve their recovery program. Students who are secretive about use must leave the school. When this occurs, often the student will return to treatment and recovery and may return to the school after that.

In the past, confidentiality rules prohibited the staff from saying why "John" is no longer attending the academy. "That created a lot of angst and anger with the students," explained language arts teacher Angela Wilcox. Rumors would fly, and students would accuse staff of not being fair to classmates who were expelled.

Now if a student uses and is open about it, a condition of the plan to stay in school is to hold a circle with the entire student body. Everyone participates as the student talks about what has happened. If a student must leave the school due to relapse, they have an option: They can leave without a circle or they can leave after having a circle. That way, if a student is suddenly gone one day, students can ask, "Where is Maddy?" and the answer is "Maddy is gone and she chose not to have a circle." Everyone knows what that means but no confidentiality is broken. Students can call Maddy on their own time. The angst and rumors don't roil up.

> At PEASE, if a student uses drugs or alcohol and immediately asks for help with it, the student is able to remain at the school. A condition of the plan to stay in school is to hold a circle with the entire student body. Everyone participates as the student talks about what has happened.

These "prolapse" and relapse circles are a vital component of the school, Wilcox believes. For a youth who has to leave, it is an opportunity to tell their story, apologize and hear from the other students. Often youth will say, "I know what you are going through because I have been there. I hope you can come back in a good way. This is what I have learned from you — thank you." Students are able to share their concerns for their classmate and then let go, "which is what we try to teach them for their sobriety every day — to let go." Students return to class able to work, since they have had a chance to discuss some very challenging and painful issues.

If a student completes further treatment and their recovery is stabilized, they can return to PEASE and re-enter with another circle, where they can share what they learned and their plan for sobriety. The other students can easily welcome them, because even though they broke the rule and left the school, the relationships were not broken.

Circle is not group therapy, says Wilcox and others who use the process with youth who are or have been in treatment. It is a communication process where everyone is respected, listened to and can participate. Participants sit in a circle, and a keeper or facilitator (either staff or student) opens the circle, welcomes everyone and passes a talking piece. The person who has the talking piece gets to speak, hold it in silence or pass it on. Everyone else gets to listen. "There is a tremendous amount of permission given to a youth to talk when they have a tangible, physical object in their hands," says Cordelia Anderson, one of the trainers for the Academy staff. "Quiet students," said Wilcox, "even students new to the school that morning will speak when they get the talking piece."

Wilcox describes the process as one that honors every voice and gives time to every student. Everyone is heard, everyone listens. It is because of the respect and safety of the process that so many students who are being expelled ask for a circle and perhaps why expelled students often return. The process is hard, though, especially for the relapsing youth.

Although the process can have strong therapeutic value, Anderson — a therapist herself — sees that there are significant differences between circle and group therapy. In a circle, the hierarchy is flat and the process is not led by a therapist. With the passing of the talking piece in an orderly manner around the circle, there are no back and forth confrontational dialogues. In therapy, some voices can dominate (although a skilled therapist can mitigate that), while in a circle all have a turn to be heard, and there is more listening and reflecting.

Kay Pranis, formerly with the Minnesota Department of Corrections Restorative Justice Unit, posed the question about circle and therapy group to both adults and youth as part of circle training at the Red Wing Correctional Facility (which has separate units for male juvenile and adult offenders), in Red Wing, Minnesota. While the adults all thought circle was just like group, the youth very clearly noted distinctions. They spoke of the power of the therapist over the youth in group. Said Pranis, "When someone has power over you — to get to another level in the facility, to get extra privileges, to ultimately get released — your behavior is to that power. The young men talked about offering phony behavior in group because they were trying to get to the next level."

Pranis continued, "The people facilitating therapy groups have good intentions and are working within professional protocols and frameworks. But sometimes they don't recognize that the kid is speaking to the power and not to the truth. Or they recognize the youth is not speaking the truth but don't know how to get around that problem." In circle the youth felt they could speak truthfully because all were treated equally, people could pass without some serious consequence, and confrontation was replaced by deeper listening. It was a safe place.

The PEASE chemical dependency counselor does conduct group therapy in a separate sobriety group, and she sees the two processes as complementary but different. The counselor arranges the prolapse and relapse circles, in that she calls everyone together. Once assembled, however, she says to the group, "Kurt wants to hold a

Students participate in a circle, an essential community-building process at PEASE Academy.

circle" and hands the talking piece to the student. The student opens the circle, explains why they are all there and passes the piece to the group. Staff and students in the circle share their comments, observations, insights, disappointments and encouragement. The student also closes the circle.

In these circles there can be "70 people in the circle — everyone is patient," says Wilcox. "It feels like the circle belongs to everyone who is in it. No one person is in control, and there are no predictable outcomes. Insight and tone can come from the most surprising people."

In the past they held group meetings where students confronted each other on suspected use, but from Wilcox's observations, they seemed much less healthy, more like a witch hunt. With the culture of circles, the students are accustomed to being heard and honored, and the edge is off, replaced by concern.

The Academy's initial three-day training in circles and restorative principles included all of the teachers, the administrative assistant and the staff person for the church facility they use, a community liaison from the neighborhood where the school is located and the special education teacher assigned to the school from the Minneapolis School District, 14 people in all.

The small size of the school allowed for an easier application of the ideas and process, as did the 100 percent buy-in by staff. "There was not a second's hesitation on the part of the staff," said Wilcox. "This program at the school is a natural fit for circle work. Students come to us from treatment. They are used to sitting in groups and sharing feelings."

"If the chemical dependency counselor comes to the fifth-hour class and says, 'We need to have a circle,' we will all go," says Wilcox. "Every teacher knows that in the long term, the circle saves time and energy. It is worth it to take the time."

The circle process is also used to repair other harms, like a fight, angry words or a problematic classroom situation, and to address conflicts between students. The staff also called a circle for themselves to meet with the board of directors and to start the new school year by addressing issues left over from the previous year's work. Noted Wilcox, "We would be hypocrites if we didn't do this ourselves."

13

Sefton Centre
for Restorative Practice
....
Creating a Restorative Community

BY LAURA MIRSKY

T
he Sefton Centre for Restorative Practice has a goal — to create a restorative community. The brainchild of Sefton Youth Offending Team (YOT) manager Steve Eyre, the center may be the only building in the UK dedicated to restorative practices. (There are 154 multiagency YOTs under the guidance of the Youth Justice Board in all of the local authorities in England and Wales, made up of representatives from probation, education, social services, health and police. Their principal aim is to stop and prevent young people from committing offenses by providing programs and interventions to both the court and the young offenders themselves.)

For nearly two years, with training and assistance from IIRP UK, the center's team — including Eyre, line manager John Gibbens, restorative justice facilitator Paul Moran, restorative justice development officers Mark Finnis and Paula Downes, police officer

Malcolm McConchie, senior prevention manager Carol Jenkinson, victim inclusion officers Sylvia Bouqdib and Sharon Jones and support staffer Carla Cunningham — has been implementing restorative practices across the board in Sefton.

The team has brought restorative practices training and support to hundreds of education, social work and criminal justice personnel in schools, the youth justice sector, looked-after children's homes (for children subject to care orders for various reasons) and neighborhoods. Said Eyre, "If there's one principle that we're trying to adhere to, it's to view restorative practices as a way of life." Added Gibbens, "One of my aims is to make restorative practices indispensable — to link it to the government's preventive agenda."

A borough with a population of about 300,000 on the northwest coast of England, Sefton is quite diverse, encompassing some of the most deprived communities in northern Europe, such as Bootle, as well as very affluent areas, such as Formby and Southport. Many of the restorative practices efforts have focused on the more disadvantaged areas, and the most extensive of that is happening in schools. "I decided early days that I wanted to work within schools and that's really what's made a big difference here," said Eyre.

> "Restorative practices works on the corridors, it works in the playground. You can bring parents in. You can bring everybody that's affected by the situation to tell the child how they feel, how it's affecting their life. We never did that before. An absolutely brilliant concept."
>
> — Judith Rankin

According to Mark Finnis, the center is delivering restorative practices training and support to staff and students at 35 of Sefton's 110 primary and secondary schools. Director of IIRP UK Les Davey said that staff at these schools have had the full four-day IIRP UK Accredited Facilitator Skills Training course, which covers the informal use of restorative practices, restorative conferencing with and without victims present and more. Some have also received the SaferSanerSchools Introduction to Restorative Practices day.

Secondary school students are being trained in restorative practices, too, said Finnis — to be peer mediators, to use restorative questions to help each other sort things out ("What happened?" "What were you thinking about at the time?" "What can you do to make things better?"), in listening and communication skills, body language, understanding relationships, confidentiality, child-protection (i.e., what issues are safe to talk about) and role-playing.

For a primary-school anti-bullying project, children who volunteered to be mentors or "special friends to other children" were trained "to conduct a friendship on restorative lines," said Eyre. The schools installed brightly colored "Friendship Benches" in the playgrounds. "When a kid's feeling unhappy or being bullied they just go and sit on a bench. Then one of these mentors finds them and they have a conversation. The children are solving their own problems, we hope, and learning new skills." In the term prior to this initiative, said Eyre, one primary school had 30 disruptive lunchtime incidents, and in the term following it, they had none.

Restorative conferencing is used for such school incidents as bullying, theft, assaults on staff and student fighting. Finnis talked about a conference that involved two learning mentors (who support students with emotional difficulties) and three 15-year-old boys at St. George of England High School in Bootle. "According to the school, they were three of the most challenging lads in the school — should have been excluded — but had a good relationship with these learning mentors," said Finnis. Then the boys kicked in the door of the learning mentors' office and tried to steal a laptop computer.

> "Restorative practices is proving effective with some of the more challenging pupils, particularly in the interpersonal relationship side. It encourages staff, it helps people listen, and it gives people a voice."
>
> — Steve Wilson

Finnis facilitated a conference that included the boys, and the learning mentors and the year head, who all felt terribly let down because they'd gone out of their way to support the boys. In the conference, the mentors expressed their hurt and disappointment. "The boys hadn't taken much responsibility, but within the conference they really did," said Finnis. "One of them had tears in his eyes." As part of the conference agreement, the boys were asked to remove graffiti and to volunteer at a younger boys' after-school club. "They turned up, bang on time, did double the time, cleaned all the graffiti" and volunteered at the boys' club, said Finnis. "Their relationship with the learning mentors had been repaired, and the school saw them differently. They'd always let people down, and now they'd actually followed

Sefton Centre team members pictured here are (from left) Carol Jenkinson, Mark Finnis, John Gibbens, Sylvia Bonqdib, Paul Moran and Sharon Jones. Additional team members not shown are Paula Downes and Steve Eyre.

through with something and were really sorry. Every year they have a school disco, and every year before they attended drunk and under the influence of drugs and caused a heap of carnage. But about three months after the conference they attended their final one, at a really posh hotel. The school were really worried and were going to tell them that they weren't allowed to come, but because of the conference, they saw them in a different light. So these three lads attended and stayed sober and were really good throughout. They also finished school without being thrown out." Added Finnis, "It's better to build bridges than brick walls."

In 20 schools in the most deprived areas of Sefton (including Bootle), the Sefton Centre has partnered with the Behaviour Improvement Programme (BIP) of the Department for Education and Skills of England

and Wales. Under the auspices of BIP manager Helen Flanagan, the BIP supplemented the YOT's funding to bring restorative practices to these schools. Flanagan believes that restorative practices fits well with approaches that the BIP has introduced, including solution-focused therapy and improving emotional literacy, saying, "Sometimes where a child has done something that's harmed someone else, while we can look at it in a solution-focused way, the harmed person needs a voice and the wrongdoer needs to know the effects if we're going to be truly emotionally literate."

Students at St. James Primary School participate in a restorative circle facilitated by Mark Finnis, restorative justice development officer at the Sefton Centre for Restorative Practice.

In these 20 schools, permanent exclusions have been reduced by 70 percent since 2003. Said Flanagan, "The schools are saying, 'Before we will consider an exclusion, if there is a very serious incident, we will conference it first and then monitor it.'" Recidivism has been reduced as well. "We've run 50 conferences this term among the 20 schools and there has been no recidivism for bullying or assaults on or swearing at teaching staff," she said.

It's also clear that a change in culture has occurred in the Sefton schools that have introduced restorative practices. Eyre said that the government's Office of Standards in Education, which he described as "tough, top-down and rigorous," wrote a report noting the "evident change in the atmosphere in the schools they visited since we've been involved." He added, "It's not just about behavior: It's a far more positive learning environment for the kids, a happier, more relaxed school, where the kids can engage with education more successfully."

School staff seem keen on restorative practices. Said Judith Rankin, Bootle High School learning support manager, "It works on the corridors, it works in the playground. It is actually seeping through. You can bring parents in. You can bring everybody that's affected by the situation to tell the child how they feel, how it's affecting their life. We never did that before. An absolutely brilliant concept."

Steve Wilson, deputy head teacher, St. George of England High School, said, "We are the sort of school that always has to be looking for initiatives that might help and support our pupils. It's proving effective with some of the more challenging pupils, particularly in the interpersonal relationship side. It encourages staff, it helps people listen and it gives people a voice, even at the lowest level. The impression from pupils is that 'someone at least is letting me have my say.' It seems to have taken the confrontation out of situations, because victim and perpetrator both feel that they've had a fair airing. With bullying, one thing the victim always wants to know is that they'll be safe and it won't happen again."

The Sefton Centre has attracted attention from leaders in the UK's restorative justice movement. Sir Charles Pollard, board member of the Youth Justice Board for England and Wales, formerly chief constable of the Thames Valley Police, said, "We've been looking over here for an example of an RJ approach in schools that was not just one school but a whole group of schools where they've really implemented it well, and therefore you can see what the results should be when you do it properly."

Pollard views the decrease in school exclusions as vitally important to reducing youth crime. "After permanent exclusions, you've lost them. They're on the street and much more likely to be getting into trouble with the law. Whenever a school excludes a student, the cost to the school is huge, about £1,000. Apart from keeping thousands of young people in school, it would save the government millions. That's merely the cost of exclusion, nothing about the cost of having young people on the streets, committing crime, taking drugs, having very unhappy lives, all the impact on public services in the future. The cost of that would be billions."

Pollard values Sefton's implementation model because it employs a multiagency team, highly trained as both practitioners and trainers, working full-time, with funding to enable them to run low-cost training courses quickly and effectively. "If you've got a core of people trained to a high level of professionalism in RJ working together, some really good learning can go on. The standards increase and people get better and share experiences and practice. There's a critical mass where if you do that, you really do move forward very fast and very well in RJ," he said, adding, "I know enough about RJ to recognize something good in Sefton."

Youth Justice Board member Graham Robb, a former head teacher who works within the Behaviour and Attendance Division of the Department for Children, Schools and Families of England and Wales, with a particular focus on reducing violence in schools, concurs with Pollard on Sefton's success: "First of all it's in a multiagency setting, and secondly, there's the impact on exclusion. And I think it's really important that it's not just one school trying to do this on its own."

"We need to build on our own success now," concluded line manager John Gibbens. "We took an off-the-shelf training package and delivered it. Fortunately it was the IIRP training. You need to get a group believing it and that's what we've done. We called ourselves a center and got a building in the middle of town, so people have an image then. We're a team."

14

Restorative Approaches
in Scottish Schools

Transformations and Challenges

By Gwynedd Lloyd, Jean Kane, Gillean McCluskey,
Sheila Riddell, Joan Stead and Elisabet Weedon

Scotland, a small country with a population of 5,054,800, is a semi-autonomous part of the UK with its own parliament, responsible for policy on education, social welfare, justice and the environment. A third of Scottish children live in families whose average income is less than 50 percent of the British average income.

There are contradictions within Scottish approaches to justice with, for Europe, a relatively high level of adult prisoners, alongside more liberal policies of community service and restorative justice. The Scottish Children's Hearing System provides a strong background to the development both of restorative youth justice and of restorative approaches in schools. This system deals with children and young people in terms of their identified need, rather than their actions — dealing with the "depraved and the deprived" together. The focus of decision making is clearly on the welfare of the child. This combined approach to welfare and offending remains strong in Scotland, in the face of what has been described as the international retreat from welfare (Hallett and Hazel, 1998).

A key finding from a range of research indicates a strong link and overlap in the lives of children between victimization/care issues and offending. This raises some issues for approaches to restorative practice that focus strongly on the idea of harm, concentrating practices on the idea of distinctively separate victims and offenders (Lloyd, et al, forthcoming).

Most Scottish councils now have youth restorative justice projects; practices include restorative justice conferences, face-to-face meetings, shuttle dialogue, police restorative warnings, support for persons harmed, victim awareness and restorative conversations.

RESTORATIVE APPROACHES IN SCOTTISH EDUCATION — THE EDUCATIONAL CONTEXT

Most children in Scotland attend neighborhood elementary and comprehensive (i.e., nonselective) high schools. Four percent attend private fee-paying schools. About two percent are educated in special schools and mainstream units for additional support for learning. This is a fairly constant figure despite policies of inclusion/mainstreaming. Compulsory schooling is from age 5 to 16, with a subsequent rate of about 15 percent of young people age 16-plus not in work, education or training.

Significant issues in recent years echo those in other countries, such as England and the USA, with a strong standards agenda, concerns about multiple policy innovation, about the impact on classrooms of policies of inclusion and over what are often perceived to be declining standards of students' behavior (Munn, 2004). The main education legislation emphasizes the right of students to a school education and an overall presumption of mainstream educational placement. Recent legislation uses a broad, functional and interactive definition of additional support needs, recognizing that these derive from barriers to learning that may be institutional and pedagogical, as well as individual. However, this policy move away from "deficit" models is paradoxically paralleled by an increasing move toward the medicalization of children's behavior, through growing diagnoses, for example, of attention deficit hyperactivity disorder (Lloyd, 2006). Recent curriculum guidelines have moved toward a re-emphasis on teacher autonomy and curricular flexibility.

A survey of teachers' views in 2004 found the majority of students to be well-behaved, though an increasing number of teachers encountered a wide range of potentially disruptive behavior in the classroom and around the school. Low-level disruption continued to be the most wearing for teachers; growing numbers reported physical aggression by students but not a major problem of violence. Gender is a constant dimension, with teachers finding boys consistently more challenging (Munn, 2004; Lloyd, 2005).

Previous policy initiatives meant that schools already offered a range of supportive practices including:
· Classroom management initiatives
· Buddy/teacher support schemes

- Circle time
- Mediation/peer mediation
- Solution-focused interventions
- Counseling skills work
- Counseling groupwork/circles
- Social skills programs
- Anger/conflict management
- Staged intervention/support schemes
- Literacy/empathy development
- Person-centered planning

Not all of these are to be found in every school; indeed, there is very considerable variation in the degree and character of student support between schools and between local councils.

THE SCOTTISH PILOT PROJECTS ON RESTORATIVE PRACTICES/APPROACHES

The Scottish Executive (government) provided funding for a 30-month pilot project in three Scottish councils (recently extended by a further two years). The overall aim for the pilot projects was to learn more about restorative practices in school settings and to look at whether there could be a distinctive Scottish approach, that is, an approach that both complemented and offered something additional to Scottish practice.

The three pilot councils have developed their restorative projects in different ways, although they have worked with the Scottish Executive to develop a broadly common underpinning philosophy. The development of these projects reflects a political will to develop practical approaches, in partnership with practitioners in the field:

to allow the pilots to be developmental, the national initiative to be highly participative and the evaluation to be formative. Eighteen schools were identified as pilot evaluation schools; these include ten high schools, seven elementary schools and one special school, in urban, suburban and rural areas and in areas of severe economic poverty as well as areas of relative economic wealth. They had varied histories in terms of existing approaches that could be described as restorative and had very varied expectations of the project. A two-year formative evaluation of the work was contracted, to be conducted by the universities of Edinburgh and Glasgow. This evaluation is now almost complete.

The pilot and the evaluation both began in 2004. The pilot sought to work with councils and schools in an iterative process over the more than two-year period of the evaluation. It involved working with staff in the three councils to clarify the nature and goals of the pilot initiatives and develop a methodology for the evaluation, in which participants as well as researchers played a critical part.

The evaluation involved the collection of a wide range of qualitative data through formal and informal interviews, focus groups, observation in classrooms and meetings, as well as more quantitative methods, such as staff and pupil surveys, and the collection of hard data, such as numbers of pupils expelled. At every stage we fed back and discussed with school managers, key personnel and council administrators, and so the evaluation process evolved in response to their concerns. We set out in each of the 18 schools to evaluate their own distinctive aims and to gather data common to all the schools.

The Scottish Framework for
Restorative Practices/Approaches

The terms "restorative practices" and "restorative approaches" are used in education to mean restoring good relationships when there has been conflict or harm and developing school ethos, policies and procedures that reduce the possibilities of such conflict and harm. They are approaches that acknowledge that schooling is an increasingly complex task, with increasingly wider demands on schools in a diverse and complex world and that teachers' work can be challenging and stressful. The Scottish projects varied in their language, using restorative "practice," "interventions" or "approaches." We have argued elsewhere that the concept of restorative approaches can offer a much more relevant focus for thinking about conflict, about change and about schools as learning communities. From now on I am going to use restorative approaches; however, this should not obscure the fact that the terminology does vary in Scotland.

Both the Executive and the councils were keen to emphasize that restorative approaches should be seen, not so much as an entirely new approach for innovation-stressed schools, but as one that offers a framework within which existing good practice can build and develop; it also adds a new dimension to thinking and practice for inclusion.

Restorative approaches were seen to involve a set of principles, strategies and skills. The underpinning principles included:

· The importance of fostering social relationships in a school community of mutual engagement

- Responsibility and accountability for one's own actions and their impact on others
- Respect for other people, their views and feelings
- Empathy with the feelings of others affected by one's own actions
- Fairness
- Commitment to equitable process
- Active involvement of everyone in school with decisions about their own lives
- Issues of conflict returned to the participants, rather than behavior pathologized
- A willingness to create opportunities for reflective change in students and staff

The Scottish approach acknowledges the theoretical framework underpinning other approaches to supporting children in schools. These include humanistic, person-centered psychology, cognitive-behavioral approaches, the "social model" and sociological perspectives on social and educational processes that recognize conflicting purposes of schooling. (Likewise the developing theoretical model on restorative justice in Scotland draws less on criminological perspectives on harm/shame and more on person-centered and cognitive perspectives. See www.restorativejusticescotland. org.uk.) Thus, restorative approaches recognize the human wish to feel safe, to belong, to be respected and to understand and have positive relationships with others. They acknowledge the potential of social and experiential learning approaches that enable students (and staff) to understand and learn to manage their own behavior. They recognize the fundamental importance of both effective support and clear control and boundaries in schools.

Practices seen in the pilot schools ranged on the continuum from whole-school approaches to those used in more challenging situations or with individual students. They included:
· Restorative ethos building
· Curriculum focus on relationship development/conflict prevention
· Restorative language
· Restorative conversations
· Checking-in circles
· Problem-solving circles — small or whole-class
· Mediation, shuttle mediation and peer mediation
· Restorative meetings or small conferences
· Restorative management of exclusion/reintegration
· Few formal conferences

Related complementary developments, seen by schools to be part of their restorative approaches initiative, included:
· School playground activities/games
· Social skills/conflict-prevention programs, e.g., Cool in School

In Scotland there has been little emphasis on the use of external facilitators in schools, but rather a commitment to the training and skills development of school staff and students.

Both the Executive and the councils recognized the need for staff development and continuing support for practice. Early in the pilots a number of staff from two of the councils visited the IIRP, in Bethlehem, Pennsylvania,

USA, and colleagues from Bethlehem have subsequently delivered a range of courses for council staff. The English organization Transforming Conflict has been heavily involved in council staff development; Marg Thorsborne and Peta Blood from Australia have given a range of seminars. So there has been an international influence on practice within the context of a distinctively Scottish framework! Some staff from the pilot schools were clearly inspired and enthused by their training. Several school principals described their training as transformational and were sustaining their enthusiasm in the process of developing their schools.

OVERALL FINDINGS — DID IT WORK?

The 18 schools progressed at different speeds, elementary schools in general finding it easier to develop whole-school approaches. In every school, as expected, staff were at different stages of knowledge and commitment; in some, most were strongly involved and there was a sense of critical mass, of changing culture and ethos. However, the evaluation was able to identify real strengths and achievements across all councils and schools.

In all schools there was evidence of strong enthusiasm and commitment on the part of key staff and, in some, of real transformation of thinking and practice. Visible commitment on the part of school managers and key enthusiasts was highly significant in promoting changing practice — other interviewees identified modeling by senior and key staff as central to their own development.

Students and staff, particularly in elementary schools, identified measurable improvements in school climate and student behavior. They described restorative language in use by staff and students. In one school, visitors commented on the air of calmness. Students felt valued by staff and were able to identify restorative elements in their teachers' actions. In elementary schools where there had been a focus on conflict prevention and mediation, students had a clear understanding of how these processes worked and talked of applying the principles in their families and peer groups. In elementary schools, students spoke of being listened to by staff. Students were enthusiastic about the use of circles and restorative meetings in helping to resolve conflict.

Elementary schools had not made much use of disciplinary expulsion, but where they had this was eliminated or significantly reduced, and there was clear evidence of reduction in referrals to managers for discipline and in some cases a reduction of the need for external behavior support.

"Now it's OK to be seen [by other staff], to be talking things through — not necessary to be seen to punish." — Teacher

The high schools were more diverse in their achievements. Several had recent critical external evaluation and changes in principals that slowed the process of change. However, here, too, there was clear evidence of changing cultures and practice. In some there was still a significant challenge from a minority of resistant staff; in one school there were strong feelings by a vocal minority that this kind of approach represented an undermining of proper discipline. In others, however, there was clear evidence of a school "turning around," with significant reduction in use of punishments and of expulsion. In most high schools, staff had substituted restorative processes for more traditional punishments such as "lines," although in some, former punishment processes still remained alongside them.

FROM CONFERENCES TO CONVERSATIONS — MOVES TOWARD A BROADER APPROACH IN SCOTLAND

There were a number of significant issues identified, including the questions of consistency and sustainability.

"There's always the risk that when the going gets tough, restorative is an easy target in any school. … You've got a kind of default setting among teachers saying 'Well, that's all very well but we're not punitive enough, we're not scary enough. The kids aren't frightened of us.'" — *Staff member*

Important questions were also raised about the balance and relationship between restorative approaches and punishment, including the recognition that interventions intended to be restorative may be experienced as punitive. In some schools, particularly but not exclusively in disadvantaged areas, the culture of the neighborhood promoted "fighting back." Some schools were working hard to involve parents. In high schools there were issues about the involvement of subject teachers in restorative processes. In elementary schools there was wide recognition that restorative approaches were for everyone — staff and all students — whereas in high schools some subject staff needed to be convinced that they should be involved and that this was not simply a matter for guidance personnel and staff with discipline responsibilities.

FUTURE OF RESTORATIVE APPROACHES IN SCOTLAND

Our evaluation provides evidence of real transformation of thinking and practice in some schools and significant change across all the schools, albeit at varying pace and with resistance to a greater or lesser extent. Enthusiasm and commitment was apparent in all the schools and councils involved. The Scottish education minister has given public support. He has visited a range of schools and gave a recent talk to a national seminar without notes, indicating a real knowledge of restorative approaches. Of course in politics, education ministers change, and new ministers often wish to make their mark. However, there is significant policy support at the moment, with continued funding for the pilot schools. Other councils are developing their own approaches.

This may not be the only "answer" to issues of relationships and discipline in schools, and some of the elements may not be entirely new. However, our evaluation indicates that it has a great deal to offer. Restorative approaches can be seen to work at all levels of the school, with all students, including those in trouble or conflict. It can be seen to support staff as well as students and is nonpathologizing — students do not need to be labeled. It promotes student and staff participation in school processes, promoting the student voice. It includes elements of practice that are familiar to those of us who have been involved in educational communities, who have done circle time or social group work, and this is a strength in that some of the skills and strategies are already in use in schools. However, the new overall concept, the structuring of the skills and strategies into a coherent framework underpinned by a strong value base clearly offers something distinctive that schools can be enthusiastic about and can use as a basis to renew and develop their culture and relationships.

REFERENCES

Kane, J., Lloyd, G., McCluskey, G., Riddell, S., Stead, J. & Weedon, E. (2006). Restorative Practices in Three Scottish Councils (an evaluation funded by the Scottish Executive Education Department. Final report). Edinburgh: SEED.

Lloyd, G. (Ed.). (2005). "Problem" Girls. London: Routledge.

Lloyd, G., Stead, J., & Cohen, D. (Eds.). (2006). Critical New Perspectives on ADHD. London: Routledge.

Lloyd, G., McCluskey, G., Kane, J., Riddell, S., Stead, J. & Weedon, E. (in press). Restorative Approaches in Schools — A Distinctively Scottish Approach? In Restoring Safe School Communities: International Perspectives. Devon: Willan Publishing.

Munn, P., Johnstone, M., & Sharp, S. (2004). Teachers' Perceptions of Discipline in Scottish Schools. [Electronic version.] Scottish Executive Education Department: Insight, 15.

15

Restorative Practices
in Australia's Schools

Strong Relationships and Multischool Summits Help Schools "Be and Learn" Together

By Lynn M. Welden

Two Australian educators are making an important difference in the emotional and academic vitality of the schools in their regions. Lyn Doppler has been principal of the award-winning Rozelle Public School in Sydney, New South Wales, since 2002. Lesley Oliver is manager of Student Inclusion and Wellbeing for the government of South Australia's Department of Education and Children's Services (DECS), representing the South West (SW) Metro District of Adelaide. Each has been recognized for her leadership role in embedding restorative practices in Australian schools.

Restorative practices (RP) in schools is based on the principles of restorative justice. Police officer Terry O'Connell was one of the restorative justice pioneers in Australia in the early 1990s. Currently director of Real Justice Australia (an affiliate of the International Institute for Restorative Practices), Terry O'Connell found that bringing offenders and victims and their supporters together in a face-to-face meeting had a beneficial effect on the healing process. His "scripted model," used in facilitating such restorative conferences, has had enormous impact on criminal justice throughout the world.

In 1996 O'Connell began to adopt restorative justice concepts for use in the classroom. RP is now employed by an increasing number of public and religious schools in New South Wales, South Australia and Victoria. Doppler, in Sydney, and Oliver, in Adelaide, worked closely with O'Connell to introduce RP at their respective sites.

"It's rare that a school within South Australia today is not aware of RP," said Oliver. "Each district has some schools using RP principles." Doppler agreed: "Though we're doing our things in different ways, we're always interested in learning about what each other is doing."

In 2004, about 10 schools in inner-city Sydney, including Rozelle, received RP training from O'Connell. This included students, staff and parents. "All stakeholders 'singing from the same book' are essential to the sustainability of the RP paradigm," said Doppler.

Within two years, Rozelle had experienced a culture change and notable improvements — higher test scores, increased community connectedness, increased enrollments, high parent participation and a decrease in suspensions and bullying. Under Doppler's guidance, the school has assumed responsibility for empowering all stakeholders and respecting diversity. A top priority became closing the gap in learning for Aboriginal students, who compose 4 percent of the student population, and the 34 percent of students who did not speak English as a first language. Acknowledging individuals' cultural backgrounds in a restorative way has strength-ened the identity of indigenous students and those from immigrant backgrounds. These students' parents also feel more valued, especially when consulted about their children's academic goals.

Rozelle School was awarded the prestigious Director-General's Award for Outstanding Achievement in Being and Learning Together in 2006. Doppler received a Winston Churchill Fellowship the same year, granting her the opportunity "to study the effects of student achieve-ment in schools where RP has been embedded as a way of learning and being together — in the UK, USA and Canada."

> "Restorative practices is a multifaceted and respectful way of being that instills trust and a sense of hope."
>
> — Lesley Oliver

Doppler's fellowship report findings reinforce the strong link between behavioral change and academic achievement she experienced at Rozelle. "Restorative practices can become a way of sensing the soul of a school," Doppler said. "During my travels, I could tell just by walking into a school and a teacher's room what the school was like."

Doppler related the story of a mother and child who had left the Rozelle school district several years ago. The mother told the principal at her child's new school, "Your school is lovely, but there's something missing," and informed her about Rozelle and how RP had built such a nurturing environment there. The principal re-mained unconvinced. Eventually the mother and child moved back to the Rozelle district. Recently, however, that same principal wrote Doppler inquiring about how to implement RP, saying, "There is something missing and I need to address it."

Lesley Oliver turned to RP and O'Connell in 2005 in response to behavioral problems within the SW Metro schools. "What we were doing wasn't working. Teachers were pursuing a very authoritarian way of dealing with students," she said. "Restorative practices offered an alternative: a way of being, centered on building good relationships. We began working with students to establish a sense of responsibility and accountability. This multifaceted and respectful way of being instilled trust and a sense of hope."

West Beach Public School pupils and teacher Rosemary Griffin participate in SW Metro District's Restorative Directions Day, engaging in a circle process.

"You build effective classroom governance by encouraging students to build the capacity for self-knowledge," said O'Connell. "Fundamental to this process is engagement and the need to be heard and understood."

Teachers profited from a similar process of engagement. "Previously we had done things for the teachers in our district," said Oliver. "Rather than convincing teachers, we let teachers reflect. Listening and asking good questions is RP at its best. As I started to ask questions, both our teachers and my staff started resolving situations for themselves. The result was increased effectiveness and enjoyment of the work, for everyone."

Oliver and her team, mentored and supported by O'Connell, had established RP in 48 schools in the SW Metro district of Adelaide by the end of 2006. With input from her DECS colleagues (including Cheryl Bevan, student support and disability manager) and an independent researcher, Oliver began examining the effect RP had on these schools.

The preliminary research from 2006 confirmed that the introduction of RP positively impacted teacher practice in the classroom. There were several issues that affected the degree of influence, including "philosophical agreement with the [RP] model, depth of understanding of the model, leadership, resourcing, opportunities for practice, reflection and peer support."

Evaluations done in 2007 demonstrated how supportive leadership and whole-school approaches advanced the process of embedding RP in the schools. Additional data showed a decrease in expulsions, suspensions, detentions and absences.

In mid-December of 2006, Oliver and district leadership asked, "What's next?" To learn how they could sustain their progress and ensure its growth, the team launched multiple school summit meetings, where sites would share stories of their RP journeys, learn from each other's successes and setbacks, forge beneficial connections and strategize for the future.

The initial two SW Metro district summits took place in March and June 2007. The top eight schools farthest along in implementing RP were invited to participate. Key staff members from each site shared insights about how RP was benefiting their school. "Schools presenting their stories to other schools at the summit is the most powerful form of communication," said Oliver. "It's a rigorous process of reflection and review — and of tremendous value." The District Restorative Directions Day in November 2007, which was the culmination of the prior summits, allowed summit schools, represented by staff and students, to share their practice with all the schools in the district.

Kim Hebenstreit, principal of Thebarton Senior College, attended the 2007 summits. The college is one of three dedicated state-funded schools in South Australia that teach adults, many from Africa and Afghanistan, who have experienced loss and trauma. In addition to establishing valuable networks, Hebenstreit noted that the summit participants "gained confidence in our own processes."

Behavioral problems at Thebarton led Hebenstreit to invite O'Connell to facilitate a restorative conference at the college in 2005. "In teaching adults, traditional discipline measures or giving punishments like detention are inappropriate," said Hebenstreit. Several of the school's refugee students had personal issues that were resulting in explosive behavior. After making the implementation of RP a top priority, Thebarton experienced a dramatic turnaround in school culture. In 2007 it was chosen as the first secondary UN School for Global Peace in Australia.

The Sydney Region Student Services Team hosted the region's first school summit (which they called a "forum") in September 2007. One hundred representatives from more than 80 schools in the region attended. Four primary schools and secondary schools at different points in the implementation of RP shared their stories. Key speakers Lesley Oliver and Lyn Doppler reported on their work as well. Forum participants will now meet on a regular basis to problem solve and come up with innovative long-term measures to advance RP in Sydney schools.

Oliver, Doppler and other committed educators in southern Australia are creating a vital network dedicated to keeping their RP vision on track. Though in its infancy, the research and evaluation undertaken by Oliver and DECS is adding rigor and direction to RP expansion in South Australia. Doppler, in turn, is a credible ambassador for the RP principles and methods that are empowering students to become, as she said, "motivated lifelong learners and happy, effective members of the global community."

16

Supporting Pupils,
Schools and Families

*The Hampshire, UK, Family Group
Conferences in Education Project*

BY LAURA MIRSKY

The Hampshire Family Group Conference Project in Education was established in 1998 to address the needs of young people who were experiencing serious problems in the education system. One of the largest non-metropolitan counties in England, Hampshire has a population of 1.5 million and encompasses both urban and rural areas, with communities ranging from prosperous to economically depressed.

Hampshire has been an important location for the development and use of family group conferencing (FGC), also known as family group decision making (FGDM).

Family group conferencing is a restorative process that empowers families to make decisions, normally made for them by public officials, concerning the care and support of their children and other family members.

The practice of FGC began in New Zealand in youth justice and child welfare applications and has spread throughout the world. In New Zealand, FGC is built into youth justice law and its use is spreading to adult cases, as well.

The key features of the New Zealand FGC model are: Prior to holding a Family Group Conference meeting, a coordinator or facilitator thoroughly prepares as many extended family members and friends as possible regarding the issues at hand to engage and inform them about the conference. At the conference, professionals (such as educators, social workers, case workers and criminal justice professionals) share information with the family group about the issues. After this portion of the conference, the family group meets by themselves, without professionals present, in a process called "family alone time" or "private family time," to develop a plan concerning the case. Subsequently, the professionals return to the meeting to assess the family's plan for safety and legal concerns. After the conference, professionals monitor and review the plan's progress and often one or more follow-up conferences are held.

There has been a wide variety of FGC activity in Hampshire County. Starting in the area of child welfare, FGC has moved into youth justice, education and domestic violence applications, among others.

The Hampshire County Council (a government organization) has been at the forefront of the development of family group conferences in the UK, and has now had more than 1,000 referrals for its innovative use of FGCs in education settings.

One of the largest counties in the UK, Hampshire has 540 schools. Although it has "an external image of leafy affluence, it also has pockets of extreme deprivation," including an Educational Action Zone of high-priority need, said Liz Holton, project manager, Family Group Conferencing, Hampshire County Education Department.

The FGC model has proved to be as valuable with well-off families as it is with those that are more deprived, said Holton, who called the project "an education-funded and -based project using the New Zealand model to promote home-school partnerships."

Children were referred to the project by staff within the education system. Referral could be for any problem relating to school, including behavioral difficulties, truancy, school phobia, bullying or being bullied and risk of temporary or permanent exclusion (also known as expulsion). Slightly less than half of the referrals were for truancy, slightly less than half for behavior problems, and the rest "a bit of both," said Holton.

Referral required a school's full agreement, indicated by a head teacher signing a referral form, thereby showing a willingness to negotiate over the family's plan and to participate in project evaluation.

In an evaluation of the first year of the pilot, in May 1999, Gill Crow, who has written and researched extensively about family group conferencing in the UK, wrote that immediate outcomes of the conferences had been positive. Teachers were found to work well with the model, and coordinators were able to transfer skills they had learned in other types of FGCs and did not require additional training. The program, now no longer in the pilot stage, has been in progress for nine years and is open to all Hampshire schools.

Holton did not note any significant difference between the child welfare and the education FGC models.

Independent coordinators — the same ones who conduct child welfare and youth justice conferences — are used: a mix of social workers and those with other types of mediation and counseling backgrounds.

The only difference in the models concerns how to schedule the conferences with respect to the school day, said Holton. Whether the FGC is held during the school day or after, both have implications for teachers. Yet teachers have responded positively to the process and have welcomed the opportunity to involve the wider family group in the child's difficulties at school.

The project has helped with ongoing communication between schools and families, said Holton, and added that Crow's research has indicated sustained improvement for six months to a year following an FGC.

One of the outstanding things about FGCs is the way they can effect small changes that have enormous impact. Holton recounted the story of a 10-year-old boy on the verge of expulsion from school whose behavior problems took up to five hours a week of his teacher's time. The boy's stepfather was terminally ill. An FGC was held, attended by the boy's mother, his biological father, the father's new partner, siblings, aunts, uncles, "the school dinner lady and even the postman," said Holton.

During the FGC, it was discovered that the boy, in addition to the rational fear of losing his dying stepfather, had an irrational fear of losing his mother. The family came up with a plan for the boy to call his mother every day from the school office to allay his fears.

The daily phone call had "a magical effect," said Holton. More support from family members was also offered at the conference, as well as professional intervention, but it was the daily phone calls that turned the tide for the boy, who was able to cope when his stepfather died.

Although a child may exhibit problems in school, it's always the tip of the iceberg, said Holton. The child may be unwanted; there may be drug or alcohol issues at home. In school FGCs, parents bring their agendas to the meetings, just as they do in child welfare FGCs. And if one child is referred for a conference, there may be similar issues for his or her siblings. If a coordinator discovers this in conference preparations, the siblings' issues will also be addressed in the conference.

FGCs in education are becoming increasingly widespread in Hampshire. Holton hopes that they will eventually be used for children with special needs and disabilities, and that the child welfare, youth justice, domestic violence and education FGC projects will all be connected. She thinks it would make more sense to have a county FGC project instead of different projects, as there is a huge amount of overlap between them. She'd also like to see families make their own referrals.

"Supporting Pupils, Schools and Families: An Evaluation of the Hampshire Family Group Conferences in Education Project," published in November 2004, by the University of Sheffield (England), Department of Sociological Studies, and Hampshire County Council Education Department, was written by Gill Crow, freelance researcher; Peter Marsh, Professor of Child and Family Welfare, University of Sheffield, and Liz Holton.

The report evaluated 50 family group conferences, carried out with a wide variety of families in 1999 and 2000 in Hampshire County schools, from implementation through many months after each conference.

The FGCs aimed to help young people aged 5 to 16 with behavior and attendance problems, but often addressed family and welfare issues, as well.

Outcomes were significantly positive. In more than half of the situations referred to FGCs, the young people's problems improved, even in serious cases.

A plan was agreed by participants in 95 percent of the FGCs, and all plans included help and support from the family group.

Approximately half of the children showed improvement with respect to both attendance and behavioral problems one month after the FGC, and between a third and half maintained the improvement six months later.

Ninety percent of both school professionals and family members said they would recommend FGCs to others, and young people said that they found the FGCs to be helpful.

Some Comments from Participants

From a family member: "I felt there was a lot of people willing to support the young person."

From a young person: "They hardly speak directly to me at school. They did much more at the meeting."

From a school professional: "It took us from the brink of permanent exclusion [expulsion] to a more stable co-operative relationship with the family."

The full report can be downloaded at www.petermarsh.staff.shef.ac.uk/F_fgcie.htm or www.hants.gov.uk/TC/edews/Reports.html.

17

APA Report Challenges
School Zero–Tolerance Policies
and Supports Restorative Justice

BY DOUGLAS GRAVES AND LAURA MIRSKY

A report issued by the American Psychological Association (APA) at their summer 2006 annual meeting found that zero-tolerance policies in use throughout U.S. school districts have not been effective in reducing violence or promoting learning in school. The report called for a change in these policies and indicated a need for alternatives, including restorative practices such as restorative justice conferences.

The report was written by an APA task force, led by Cecil R. Reynolds, Ph.D., of Texas A&M University, which was charged with reviewing the effectiveness of zero-tolerance policies in American schools. In essence, the report found that "zero tolerance has not been shown to improve school climate or school safety."

Although it seems intuitive that removing disruptive students from schools will improve the school experience for others and that severe punishment will improve the behavior of both the punished and those who witness the punishment, the task force report asserts that the available evidence "consistently flies in the face of these beliefs."

Indeed, the task force found that zero-tolerance polices may have actually increased disciplinary problems and dropout rates in middle and secondary schools, exacerbated the problem of overrepresentation of minority and emotionally disabled students in school discipline systems, and generated inappropriate consequences for younger children.

The American Psychological Association (APA), in Washington, D.C., is the largest scientific and professional organization representing psychology in the United States and is the world's largest association of psychologists. APA's membership includes more than 150,000 researchers, educators, clinicians, consultants and students. Through its divisions in 54 subfields of psychology and affiliations with 60 state, territorial and Canadian provincial associations, APA works to advance psychology as a science, as a profession and as a means of promoting health, education and human welfare (from www.apa.org).

Zero tolerance—based punishments such as suspension and expulsion, the task force found, have not improved behavior or academic performance. In addition, by shifting the locus of discipline from schools to the juvenile justice system, zero-tolerance policies are causing numerous adverse consequences for students, families and communities.

Zero-tolerance policies requiring suspension from school were found to be counterproductive on many levels: "School suspension in general appears to predict higher future rates of misbehavior and suspension among those students who are suspended."

Schools with higher rates of school suspension and expulsion had less satisfactory school climate ratings and school governance structures, and tended to spend a disproportionate amount of time on discipline. In the

long term, school suspension and expulsion were asso-
ciated with a higher school dropout rate and failure to
graduate on time.

As to academic performance, the report saw "a negative relationship between the use of school suspension
and expulsion and school- wide academic achievement."

Regarding the notion that zero-tolerance policies
might be fairer to "students traditionally over-repre-
sented in school disciplinary consequences," the task
force found that the opposite seemed to be true. Under
zero-tolerance policies "the disproportionate discipline of students of color continues to be a concern and
may be increasing; over-representation in suspension
and expulsion has been found consistently for African
American students and less consistently for Latino students." Furthermore, the study found that under zero-
tolerance policies, "African American students may be
disciplined more severely for less serious or more sub-
jective reasons."

Concerning students with disabilities, although
there is less data available on this issue, the report
found that, under zero-tolerance policies, "students
with disabilities, especially those with emotional and
behavioral disorders, appear to be suspended and expelled at rates disproportionate to their representation
in the population."

The task force found these policies to be particularly
inappropriate for younger pupils. "Zero-tolerance policies as applied appear to run counter to our best knowledge of child development," the report states, adding,
"Zero-tolerance policies can exacerbate both the nor-
mative challenges of early adolescence and the potential

mismatch between the adolescent's developmental stage and the structure of secondary schools."

Regarding how zero-tolerance policies have affected the relationship between education and the juvenile justice system, the task force found that the policies have increased the use of security technology, security personnel and profiling. However, it found no evidence that such programs result in safer schools or more satisfactory school climates.

Moreover, the task force found that zero-tolerance policies have increased referrals to the juvenile justice system for infractions that were once handled in schools, resulting in the creation of a "school-to-prison pipeline." And since it costs more to handle a child through the juvenile justice system than within the school system, said the report, "To the extent that school infractions lead to increased contact with the juvenile justice system, the cost of treatment appears to escalate dramatically."

The task force expressed concern that zero-tolerance policies, by increasing "student shame, alienation, rejection, and breaking of healthy adult bonds," exacerbate negative mental-health outcomes for youth.

Further, the task force found little confirmation that zero tolerance has provided any positive effects for families or communities, and "no evidence indicating that the policies themselves have assisted parents ... or that family units have been strengthened" through the use of the policies:

"As zero-tolerance policies by nature do not provide guidance or instruction because they focus directly on punishment, such actions often are seen as unjust and may breed distrust of adult authority figures and nurture adversarial confrontational attitudes

"By subjecting students to automatic punishments that do not take into account extenuating or mitigating circumstances, zero-tolerance policies represent a lost moment to teach children respect and a missed chance to inspire their trust of authority figures."

As an alternative to zero tolerance, the task force recommends "a meaningful approach to school discipline ... one that treats students and their families with respect throughout the process, seeks to learn from students and to nurture their learning and growth as human beings and that finds ways to bring students more deeply into the school community and the surrounding community as well." To that end, the task force advocates improving collaboration and communication between schools, parents, law enforcement personnel and jurisdictions, and juvenile justice and mental-health professionals. According to the task force, these groups need to work together to develop effective alternatives for students who challenge the disciplinary rules.

> "Zero tolerance has not been shown to improve school climate or school safety."
> — APA Task Force Report

The report suggests alternatives to zero-tolerance policies, including restorative practices such as restorative justice conferences, to prevent violence and increase the sense of school safety.

The report defines restorative justice (RJ) as "a theory of justice that emphasizes repairing the harm caused or revealed by criminal behavior." RJ programs, the report states, "involve a cooperative process that: 1) identifies crime and attempts to repair its damage, 2) includes all stakeholders to respond to acts of violence and 3) changes the traditional relationship between the offenders and the victims." In contrast to zero-tolerance policies, RJ is "designed to reconcile the perpetrators with the victims, creating a feeling of resolution and increasing a sense of safety."

Restorative justice, asserts the report, "makes a contribution to a stronger school climate by increasing student understanding of existing rules and trust in the enforcement of those rules." The report also affirmed that RJ has "yielded promising results in terms of reductions in office referrals, school suspensions and expulsions, and improved ratings on measures of school climate." Explained the report, "By reducing the likelihood of retribution or repeat offending, restorative justice may prevent the escalation of violence."

"Restorative justice programs attempt to re-establish positive relationships with adults and 'teach' understanding and empathy to those who have been violent," the report commented, adding, "Restorative and community justice programs in the school setting prioritize activities that try to reduce delinquency, find solutions to delinquent behavior, build a community capacity to respond to problem behavior without resorting to the criminal justice system, and create a safe and supportive learning environment that effectively expresses the values of the culture." The report concluded, "Emerging data suggest that restorative justice programs may represent a promising alternative to zero tolerance."

To read the APA task force report, please go to: www.apa.org/ed/cpse/zttfreport.pdf.

18

Empirical Evaluations
of a Restorative School and Treatment Milieu

BY LAURA MIRSKY AND TED WACHTEL

Community Service Foundation and Buxmont Academy (CSF Buxmont), two Pennsylvania nonprofit sister agencies, operate eight alternative school/day treatment programs for delinquent and high-risk youth in eastern Pennsylvania. CSF also operates 16 residential group homes for some of the youth who attend the schools and one transitional home for young men who have completed school. Additionally, CSF provides a highly structured supervision program for adjudicated youth who have completed inpatient drug-and-alcohol treatment, many of whom also attend the schools.

In 2000 CSF Buxmont established the International Institute for Restorative Practices (IIRP), now a graduate school that grants master's degrees and a certificate in the emerging field of restorative practices. The IIRP also provides training and consulting and sponsors international conferences in that field.

Restorative practices empowers young people in CSF Buxmont schools and programs to develop their own behavioral standards, their own classroom norms and, if they persistently misbehave as individuals, their own behavioral contracts. Conflicts and problems are addressed immediately by asking the students themselves to take responsibility for finding solutions. The young people at each of the program sites consciously build a community of support, achieving interdependency and a strong sense of responsibility and concern for one another.

"The Worst School I've Ever Been To," a film about the 1999-2000 school year at a CSF Buxmont school, clearly depicts this community of support as it traces the progress of three students — Tim, Walt and Jamie — throughout the entire school year. The film's title comes from a comment made by Tim early in the school year, saying CSF Buxmont is "the worst school I've ever been to." He especially doesn't like the "group bull----" and having to "open up and talk to people." (For more information about the film "The Worst School I've Ever Been To," please see Educational Resources, at the end of this book.)

In the years since the first CSF school opened in 1977, the staff have refined strategies that bring about positive behavior change. However, for 21 years the positive reputation of the CSF Buxmont schools, group homes and probation supervision programs was based on anecdotal evidence only. Although people told good stories about CSF Buxmont and the success of kids in the programs, the results had not been measured scientifically.

Then in 1998 CSF Buxmont sought the assistance of Paul McCold, Ph.D., then director of research for the

IIRP, later a founding faculty member of the IIRP graduate school, to undertake various empirical evaluations of the effectiveness of their strategies and philosophy in helping delinquent and at-risk young people achieve positive changes in behavior and attitude.

McCold enlisted the support of Phil Harris, Ph.D., and Peter Jones, Ph.D., at Temple University. Harris and Jones conducted a preliminary evaluability study and found, among other things, that the staff at all levels of CSF Buxmont have a philosophy that is shared and articulated consistently throughout the two organizations.

At about the same time, independent of Harris and Jones, McCold surveyed school culture in several public schools and the CSF Buxmont schools (at that time there were six CSF Buxmont schools) by asking students, parents and school staff to fill out questionnaires that included questions about their perceptions of school safety.

The results were contrary to what most people would expect. Although students who attend CSF Buxmont schools are among the most conflict-prone and violent young people from each of their schools of origin, they felt dramatically safer and more comfortable at the CSF Buxmont schools than did the students at the four public middle schools who participated in the survey. The comparison of the responses to four sample survey questions (Figure 1) illustrates how much safer young people felt at all of the CSF Buxmont schools.

In early 1999 McCold began a long-term evaluation of CSF Buxmont students with evaluative scales and protocols provided by Criminal Justice Research Center (CJRC) at Temple University. The center had been us-

School Safety
Comparing Public Middle Schools to CSF

You have to watch what you do; otherwise
other students will make fun of you.

% who agree

70%

29%

How many students at this school
sometimes are picked on by other students?

% who said
many or most

49%

16%

How often have students stolen from other
students during the last month?

% who said
4 or more

47%

24%

How often have students wrecked other
students property during the last month?

% who said
4 or more

31%

8%

▣ Public Middle Schools
○ CSF Day Treatment

Figure 1. Surveyed during the spring 2000 semester at the CSF schools
and four Pennsylvania public middle schools. Results are based on 227
students in CSF schools and 3,023 students at the public schools. All
differences shown are statistically significant at p < .001 (adapted from
*The Worst School I've Ever Been To: Empirical Evaluations of a Restorative
School and Treatment Milieu, 2002*, by Paul McCold, founding faculty,
International Institute for Restorative Practices).

ing these scales and protocols to evaluate programs for
delinquent and at-risk young people from Philadelphia
for almost a decade. The results from McCold's analysis
of the data from the first two years of the ongoing CSF
Buxmont evaluation were subsequently confirmed by an
independent analysis by Peter Jones at Temple's CJRC,
completed in June 2002.

The evaluation of the CSF Buxmont programs showed significant and positive results for all six day treatment school program sites then operated by CSF Buxmont.

The full research report and an executive summary are available at the IIRP's website, at www.iirp.org/library/erm.html.

SAMPLE

The study was based on a sample of 919 youths discharged from the six CSF Buxmont day treatment school programs between June 1, 1999 and August 30, 2001. The sample was comprised of 515 youth placed in the program by county juvenile probation departments, 88 by county children-and-youth agencies and 315 by public school districts.

PROGRAM COMPLETION

Probation-referred students were significantly more likely to complete the program satisfactorily (66%) than the school-referred (53%) and children-and-youth agency-referred students (57%). Program completion rates for delinquent youth at CSF Buxmont were twice that of comparable programs in the long-term Philadelphia study conducted by the Criminal Justice Research Center. Significantly, the restorative school/day treatment program worked just as well with so-called "tough kids" as with the "easier kids."

Youth Attitudes

Researchers conducted entry and exit interviews with students in the CSF Buxmont school/day treatment programs. The interviews included scales that measured prosocial norms and self-esteem. The youth who participated in both interviews showed a significant increase in their prosocial values. For example, the students became much more willing to take responsibility and were less likely to blame others for their misbehavior. Another example of attitude improvement is that they were much more likely to have positive regard for police officers when they left the program than when they entered. Also, those completing the program had high self-esteem scores upon discharge, regardless of their self-esteem at intake. The improvement in both measures of attitude was even greater for those spending a second year in the program (see Figure 2).

Offending and Recidivism

Researchers examined juvenile and adult court records for 96 percent of the students for the six months following discharge to determine whether they had any court petitions during that time period. Youth discharged from the program prematurely for persistent misbehavior or persistent absences were nearly twice as likely as those discharged normally to have offended or reoffended. The proportion of youth with a court petition during the six months following discharge decreased in direct relation to the number of weeks they had participated in the program. In short, the program significantly reduced offending rates, usually after the youths had spent at least three months in the program. Each week beyond

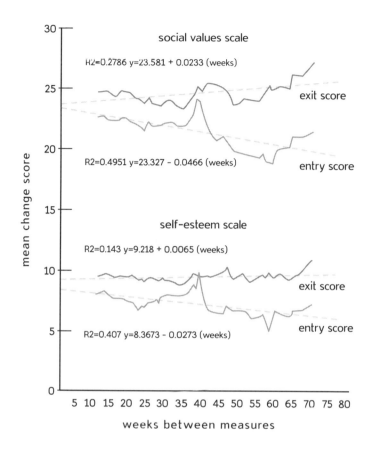

Figure 2. Average changes in prosocial norms and self-esteem measured against number number of weeks spent in the program (adapted from McCold, 2002).

the three months produced a significant further reduction in offending, with the largest decrease occurring during the fourth through sixth month of participation in the school/day treatment program, and then leveling off. Offending rates were reduced by two-thirds in six months (see Figure 3).

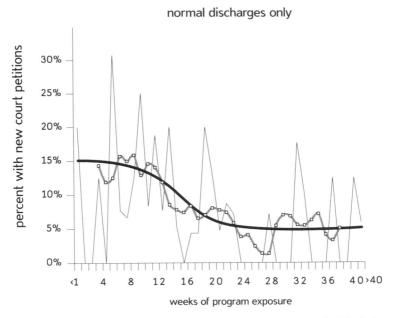

Figure 3. Offending rates relative to amount of time a student attended the program (adapted from McCold, 2002).

FOLLOW-UP STUDY

A replication and extension of the above evaluation was performed with a second wave of 858 day treatment discharges during school years 2001-02 and 2002-03. The original finding of a significant reduction in offending or reoffending for youths participating three months or more in a CSF Buxmont restorative environment was replicated with a new cohort of youths and was still evident for the original cohort at two years following discharge. To read the follow-up study, please go to: www.realjustice.org/library/erm2.html.

CONCLUSION

While similar evaluations of many programs fail to show any significant results, the empirical findings of the two CSF Buxmont studies provide strong scientific evidence that exposure to a restorative milieu positively improves both the attitudes and behavior of delinquent and at-risk youth, regardless of their age, gender, race, offense type or criminal history, and can dramatically reduce offending among at-risk and misbehaving young people.

REFERENCES

McCold, P. (2002, November). Evaluation of a restorative milieu: CSF Buxmont School/Day Treatment programs 1999-2001 evaluation outcome technical report. Paper presented at the American Society of Criminology Annual Meeting, Chicago, Illinois. [www.realjustice.org/library/erm.html]

McCold, P. (2005, January). Evaluation of a restorative milieu: replication and extension for 2001-2003 discharges. Paper presented at the American Society of Criminology Annual Meeting, Nashville, Tennessee. [www.realjustice.org/library/erm2.html]

19

Research Reveals
the Power of Restorative Practices in Schools

By Abbey J. Porter

E ducators around the globe are using restorative practices to proactively prevent problems like bullying and violence. Growing awareness that punishments such as detention and suspension only aggravate issues such as bullying, violence, poor academic performance and parental apathy has prompted educators to explore restorative practices to create safe, supportive learning environments.

As an increasing number of schools worldwide adopt restorative practices as a means of dealing with discipline and improving school culture, school leaders are beginning to analyze the impact of restorative methods. The numbers tell a powerful story: Schools implementing restorative methods have seen a drop in disciplinary problems, decreased reliance on detention and suspension and an improvement in student attitudes. Case studies and evaluations conducted in schools worldwide also indicate that restorative practices improves relationships among students and teachers and builds community. Gathering such data is important, both for evaluating the effectiveness of restorative methods and garnering funding support for restorative programs.

The most significant qualitative finding to date, said Dr. Paul McCold, founding faculty member of the International Institute for Restorative Practices (IIRP) Graduate School, is that restorative practices transform schools' academic and social culture, leading to better outcomes for students.

"We've shown in case study after case study that schools that adopt this approach report significant changes in their cultures," he said, adding, "We know that the sense of belonging and pride in school are related to academic performance and dropout rates, and dropout rates are related to involvement in the criminal justice system and more at-risk behavior. The more involvement in school and positive peer groups, the less likely students are to engage in risky behavior."

> "The only way to know that a program is effective is to evaluate it. A huge amount of money is wasted on programs that are not effective."
>
> — Dr. Paul McCold

"What's needed now is solid quantitative research," said McCold. Both quantitative and qualitative analyses are valuable, he noted, as qualitative studies can help to explain quantitative findings. Quantitative research is vital to demonstrating the impact of restorative practices, said McCold. "Otherwise, you're just following some philosophy. The only way to know that a program is effective is to evaluate it. A huge amount of money is wasted on programs that are not effective."

McCold demonstrated that restorative practices is effective even for at-risk youth by evaluating the alternative school/day treatment programs run by Community Service Foundation and Buxmont Academy, demonstration programs of the IIRP. CSF Buxmont uses restorative practices to help at-risk youth achieve positive changes in behavior and attitude.

Studies conducted from 1999 to 2003 found significant positive results: Students in the programs developed higher self-esteem and showed an increase in prosocial values, becoming more willing to take responsibility for their misbehavior. In addition, court records showed a two-thirds reduction in offending rates after six months in the program, as well as two years after discharge. (See Chapter 18, Empirical Evaluations of Restorative School and Treatment Milieu.)

> The numbers tell a powerful story: Schools implementing restorative methods have seen a drop in disciplinary problems, decreased reliance on detention and suspension and an improvement in student attitudes.

Palisades High School, in Pennsylvania, USA, was the first IIRP SaferSanerSchools pilot school, bringing the restorative practices that had been so successful at CSF Buxmont schools into a public school. Data gathered by the school showed a dramatic decrease in detentions, suspensions, disciplinary referrals and incidents of disruptive behavior from 1998–1999, when the school introduced restorative practices, to 2001–2002. Overall disciplinary referrals decreased from 1,752 to 1,154; suspensions decreased from 105 to 65; detentions dropped from 844 to 332; and incidents of disruptive behavior decreased from 273 to 153.

Restorative practices arrived at Palisades Middle School in fall 2000 via classroom circles and restorative discipline processes. Over the next year, disciplinary referrals fell from 913 to 516, and incidents of fighting dropped from 23 to 16.

Springfield Township High School, just outside Philadelphia, Pennsylvania, began implementing restorative practices in January 2000. After beginning with a small group of teachers, the entire faculty was introduced to the approach in fall 2001. Over the next year, incidents of disrespect to teachers fell from 71 to 21, and incidents of classroom disruption fell from 90 to 26. (See Chapter 4, Transforming School Culture with Restorative Practices.)

These results represent a change from a punitive to a restorative mind-set, a paradigm shift that McCold and others believe is critical. "It's widely recognized among school leaders that conventional discipline is ineffective," said Bill Sower, a Michigan, USA, schools trainer and former IIRP regional coordinator. "Out-of-school suspension rewards misbehavior for students who don't want to be in school. In-school suspension promotes the growth of negative subcultures ... which disrupt the whole school climate. Restorative practices is a credible alternative."

Restorative practices has proved effective for schools with a variety of demographics and disciplinary problems. Sower, who has trained both inner-city and suburban schools, said implementation remains essentially the same in any school environment.

In addition to improving student behavior and relationships, said Sower, restorative methods improve relationships among teachers. Before the introduction of restorative practices, Salem Elementary School, in South Lyon, Michigan, suffered from widespread discipline problems and lacked a sense of community.

Photo credit: Hal Gould, South Lyon Herald

"The teachers were very demoralized," said Sower, who used circles in a one-day training two years ago. "In the circles, teachers could express their true feelings about school culture and the distress it caused them [including] feelings of rejection or a lack of collegiality. It was a very emotional day. The staff decided to use this model in all their classes with all their students, every day."

The school implemented circles, along with occasional formal conferences for serious issues. Within a few months, teachers were reporting fewer disciplinary problems. Disciplinary referrals eventually dropped 75 percent. A 73 percent drop in disciplinary referrals at South Lyon's Centennial Middle School is also credited to restorative practices. Said Sower, "There has been a dramatic transformation in these schools regarding the level of trust and cooperation among students, between students and adults and among adults themselves. When teachers share ideas and help each other it affects the quality of instruction."

Restorative practices has also had a highly positive effect in schools in Lansing, Michigan, an urban school district. A pilot project begun in Pattengill Middle School in January 2005 introduced restorative practices to manage disciplinary issues.

At Pattengill, restorative practices:

- Supported a 15 percent drop in suspensions, while suspension rates at the district's other middle schools increased.
- Averted two expulsions.
- Resolved conflicts effectively. Ninety-three percent of 292 students participating reported using restorative methods to resolve their conflicts.
- Taught students new skills. Nearly 90 percent of participating students reported learning new skills in their restorative experiences, and 86 percent reported using those skills to peacefully resolve or avert conflicts after their restorative interventions.

The program's success led the district to expand its restorative program to one elementary school, two more middle schools and a high school in 2006–2007. Lansing restorative justice coordinator Nancy Schertzing estimated that through mid-April 2007, restorative interventions had saved Lansing students nearly 1,500 days of suspension.

In Minnesota, USA, public schools are implementing a range of restorative practices. Nancy Riestenberg, a violence prevention specialist with the Minnesota Department of Education, noted that each school is different and that restorative methods take time to implement. "You're talking about something that for a lot of people is a personal attitude and a cultural change. There's a learning curve for adults as well as children."

From 1998 through 2001, the Minnesota Department of Education conducted an evaluation of restorative practices in primary and secondary schools in four districts. The study showed a 30 to 50 percent reduction in suspensions. One elementary school reduced its behavior referrals for inappropriate physical contact from seven per day to a little more than one per day. (See Chapter 6, Restorative Practices Impacts Public Schools in Minnesota: An Interview with Nancy Riestenberg.)

Lynn Zammit, of the Waterloo Region District School Board in Ontario, Canada, believes restorative interventions interrupt the cycle of violence she has witnessed in bullying. Zammit, who coordinates the district's Choices for Youth program for expelled students, finds that offenders often start out as victims. "Many kids we see in the expulsion program have been the victims of bullying for years," she said. "They have been attacked and persecuted and isolated

> The experiences documented by restorative practices trainers, educators and researchers suggest that, while restorative practices requires time and dedication to implement, it pays off in an environment that supports positive behavior and relationships — and learning.

... until one day they make up their minds they can't take it anymore and they bring a weapon to school." Zammit wanted to reach such victims early and provide them with effective strategies.

In 2005, the Waterloo school board received a grant from the victims' services unit of the Attorney General's Office to train educators in restorative conferencing as an alternative to suspension and expulsion, as a re-entry strategy for suspended students and for classroom management.

The district's elementary suspensions dropped 80 percent in less than three years; its secondary school suspensions decreased by 65 percent; and secondary and elementary expulsions dropped by a third. Zammit said that restorative practices represents a "big part" of the district's dramatic results.

In addition to conflict resolution, restorative practices offers a compass for day-to-day interaction. "Everything to do with restorative practices is based on relationships and the need, when things go wrong, to mend relationships — and before things go wrong to stress relationships so incidents don't occur," said Zammit. She refers to "CCR — community, capacity and relationships."

> "Out-of-school suspension rewards misbehavior for students who don't want to be in school. In-school suspension promotes the growth of negative subcultures ... which disrupt the whole school climate. Restorative practices is a credible alternative."
>
> — Bill Sower

"Restorative practices is about really focusing on that sense of community, and about young people's capacity to do things differently. It's about focusing on capacities rather than deficits. When things go wrong, we hold circles and we talk and we generate solutions. It's just the way we do business here."

Zammit emphasized that circles build valuable abilities in students. "Social-emotional skills are just like any other skills; they need to be developed and modeled," she said. "Restorative practices is a means to develop empathy and kindness and caring and good communication skills." She noted that researchers such as Daniel Goleman have found that teaching social-emotional skills to children can affect long-term factors such as relationships and employment. Educators should look closely at "what trajectory we put kids on when we use punishment," she suggested.

Prior to undergoing training in restorative practices in January 2003, teachers and administrators at Queanbeyan South Public School, in New South Wales, Australia, struggled with bullying, violence and truancy among pupils. Problems were particularly prevalent among the school's Aboriginal children, many of whom came from homes that lacked support for education.

After implementation of a restorative approach, the school's detention and suspension rates and incidence of aggression against teachers dropped. The percentage of teachers reporting that they had been the subject of intimidating or threatening behavior dropped from 56 percent in 2002 to 24 percent in 2004. Teachers reporting that they had been verbally assaulted decreased from 74 percent to 61 percent, and those reporting that they had been physically assaulted plummeted from 53 percent to just 3 percent. Results were particularly striking among Aboriginal students, none of whom was suspended in 2004. These positive data have been replicated since. Queanbeyan South relief principal Rosalind Drover reported that because of their success transforming their school culture with restorative practices, theirs was one of only two government schools invited to the National Safe Schools Conference. (See Chapter 8, Restorative Practices at Queanbeyan South, an Australian Primary School.)

Marg Armstrong, an educational consultant and restorative practices trainer in Melbourne, Australia, is a former project officer with the Australian Department of Education who coordinated training in hundreds of schools. Armstrong received a Churchill Fellowship in 2004 to study restorative practices in schools in the U.S., the UK, Canada and New Zealand and has seen restorative methods reduce suspensions and detentions, increase safety and harmony and lessen stress for teachers. Said Armstrong, "If kids don't feel better about being in school, we're wasting our time. If they feel more connected to one another at school, they're going to want to be there, and if they want to be there, they're going to want to learn."

Studies involving baseline measures and comparison groups can best pinpoint the effects of implementing restorative practices in schools, noted Dr. Paul McCold. While such studies are few now, several educational and governmental groups have undertaken evaluations that demonstrate the effects of implementing restorative approaches.

A 2007 New Zealand study of five primary and secondary schools, by the Office of the Children's Commissioner and the Institute of Policy Studies at Victoria University, "Respectful Schools: Restorative Practices in Education," found restorative methods helped build respectful relationships, deal with disciplinary problems and reduce suspensions. Schools must "introduce changes across the whole school ... to improve all children's involvement and commitment to schooling." A whole-school approach is defined as commitment by students, staff, board members, family, community and government.

Time is critical. "Building a restorative community is an evolutionary process which needs everyone to be involved in a consistent application of restorative principles and practice over time," states the New Zealand report, also noting the need for long-term funding to sustain restorative approaches.

The value of whole-school commitment, along with time and resources, also emerged in a study of three primary schools in Adelaide, South Australia, conducted by the Department of Education and Children's Services. Looking at teacher and student classroom behavior in schools that implemented restorative practices in varying degrees, the study identified "clear relationships between the priority afforded to ... implementation at whole of school level and the degree of change at classroom level." Teachers at the "most restorative" school reported that students displayed less emotional volatility when dealing with issues, a stronger sense of belonging and cohesiveness, improved self-esteem and increased willingness to participate. Students in all the schools improved in communication skills, responsibility and relationships.

Between 2001 and 2004, the Youth Justice Board of England and Wales evaluated restorative programs in six primary schools and 20 secondary schools in what board member and education consultant Graham Robb considers one of the most "robustly evaluated" restorative practices projects. The schools were part of nine Youth Offending Teams, or YOTs, encompassing representatives of probation, social service, health and police.

Troubled by problems such as theft and bullying, the schools implemented a range of restorative practices, from active listening and peer mediation to restorative conferences. The study evaluated factors including participant satisfaction and the processes' impact on victimization. Secondary schools were compared to similar, "nonprogram" schools where restorative practices had not been implemented. (Nonprogram primary schools were not available for comparison.)

Surveys were conducted in the schools at the beginning and end of the implementation period. Greater improvements were evident in the three districts that had implemented restorative practices over a three-year period. Schools in the other seven districts had had only 18 months to institute restorative methods.

Among the statistically significant findings in schools where restorative practices had been implemented for three years:

- 23 percent fewer students thought that bullying was a serious problem at their school, compared to a 3-percent reduction at the nonprogram schools.
- 10 percent more students thought their school was doing a good job at stopping bullying; at nonprogram schools, 1 percent fewer students felt their school was doing a good job stopping bullying.
- The percentage of students reporting that they had never been called a racist name increased by 11 percent, compared to a 3-percent increase at nonprogram schools.

Staff surveys indicated a "significant improvement in pupil behaviour in the programme schools, while behaviour had declined in the nonprogramme schools." Staff reporting improvement in student behavior between the first survey and the follow-up survey increased by 6 percent in the program schools, compared to a decrease of 5 percent at nonprogram schools. Program school staff who reported a worsening in student behavior decreased by 9 percent, while such reporting by nonprogram-school staff increased by 12 percent.

The vast majority of restorative conferences at these schools (92 percent) resulted in successful agreements between the parties involved, and student participants reported a high degree of satisfaction (89 percent) with the conferences. Ninety-three percent said the process was fair and that justice has been done. Only 4 percent of agreements had been broken as of a three-month follow-up. Results were strongest for schools that implemented restorative practices using a whole-school approach.

Among the YOTs studied by the Youth Justice Board is the Sefton Centre for Restorative Practice. It began in 2004 to implement restorative practices across the board in the borough of Sefton, including 35 of 110 primary and secondary schools, with training conducted through IIRP UK and the IIRP's SaferSanerSchools program. In addition to training staff, children were taught to be peer mediators and to help each other sort through problems.

In 20 schools in Sefton's most deprived areas, the center partnered with the Behaviour Improvement Programme (BIP) of the Department for Education and Skills of England and Wales, which found that restorative practices fit well with its introduction of solution-based therapy and improved emotional literacy in the schools. In those 20 schools, permanent exclusions were reduced by 70 percent between 2003 and 2006. Recidivism was reduced as well. Of 59 conferences run in one term, the school experienced no recidivism for misbehavior ranging from bullying and assaults to swearing at teachers. (See Chapter 13, Sefton Centre for Restorative Practice Strives for a Restorative Community.)

The Bessels Leigh School, in Oxfordshire, England, a residential school for boys 11 to 16 with emotional and behavior difficulties, introduced restorative practices in 2004 after finding conventional punishments such as detention ineffective in dealing with its increasingly challenging clientele. The "turning point" for the school, says principal John Boulton, came in 2005 after it underwent circle training — a process that helped to create a sense of community and reduce vandalism in the school.

Comparing the three-week period in September 2004 that preceded the training to the three-week period immediately following, school officials found that negative incidents at the school dropped from 362 to 164. Negative physical incidents dropped from 13 to 9, and incidents of damage decreased from 10 to 3. (See Chapter 11, Restorative Practices and Organizational Change: The Bessels Leigh School.)

The Scottish Pilot Projects on Restorative Practices/ Approaches, begun in 2004 by the Scottish government, provided funding for a 30-month pilot project (extended by two years), bringing restorative practices to 18 schools — 10 high schools, seven elementary schools and one special school, in urban, suburban and rural areas. ("Restorative Practices/Approaches" refers to "restoring good relationships when there has been conflict or harm and developing school ethos, policies and procedures that reduce the possibilities of such conflict and harm.") A concurrent evaluation by the universities of Edinburgh and Glasgow collected qualitative data in the schools through formal and informal interviews, focus groups and classroom and meeting observation, and employed quantitative data — collection methods such as staff and pupil surveys. Hard data, such as numbers of pupils expelled, were also collected.

Gwynedd Lloyd, head of educational studies at University of Edinburgh, reported that the data were largely very positive, in terms of both the impact on observable behavior and the way restorative approaches have been received by staff and students. Lloyd noted that a whole-school restorative approach was more successful than a focus just on conferencing in response to behavioral offenses. Also, implementation was more successful when all school staff were trained in restorative approaches, as opposed to only those staff who are specifically charged with handling behavioral issues. Implementation tended to be more difficult to achieve in secondary schools than in elementary schools, possibly because secondary school teachers tend to feel the need to focus on their particular lesson or subject, rather than on educating the whole child. The government report concluded: "The evaluation indicates that restorative practices can offer a powerful and effective approach to promoting harmonious relationships in school and to the successful resolution of conflict and harm." (See Chapter 14, Restorative Approaches in Scottish Schools: Transformations and Challenges.)

School leaders who have studied the impact of restorative practices in their institutions identify another purpose for collecting data: It can help secure funding. The Lansing School District's restorative justice project, a collaborative effort with the Dispute Resolution Center of Central Michigan and the Tri-County Balanced and Restorative Justice Alliance, has secured multiyear funding from the Capital Area United Way and support from the Capital Region Community Foundation.

"We wouldn't have any grantors if we didn't have statistics showing we're actually making a difference," said Lansing's restorative justice coordinator, Nancy Schertzing. "You have to compete out there for a limited pool of funds. The data is very powerful, and it makes people take us much more seriously. It gets people's attention in a way that stories don't."

The experiences documented by restorative practices trainers, educators and researchers suggest that, while restorative practices requires time and dedication to implement, it pays off in an environment that supports positive behavior and relationships — and learning. The IIRP hopes that these encouraging results will help foster the growth of restorative practices in schools and other settings worldwide.

Educational **Resources** produced by the **IIRP**

To learn more about books, videos and other resources
provided by the IIRP, please go to **www.iirp.org/store**.

Beyond Zero Tolerance:
Restorative Practices in Schools

This 25-minute video documents the implementation of restorative practices in several schools in the USA, the Netherlands, and Hull, England. The camera captures circles, conferences and one-on-one meetings in progress. Students, teachers and administrators speak candidly about the effects of restorative practices in their schools. The involvement of parents is touched on as well. The viewer is transported to bustling school hallways and classrooms and feels an unmistakable sense of lively and cheerful community. This vibrant and engrossing video is a powerful testament to the benefits of restorative practices in an educational setting.

Roundtable Discussions #1 & #2:
Restorative Strategies for Schools

Four expert practitioners of restorative practices discuss how to address a range of disciplinary and behavioral issues in schools. An ideal tool for administrators to raise their faculty's consciousness about restorative practices. Topics discussed include attendance issues, acting out in the classroom, bullying, working with parents, restorative consequences, favorite stories and dealing with difficult situations.

The Worst School I've Ever Been To

This video follows the stories of three students — Tim, Walt and Jamie — for an entire school year at a Community Service Foundation and Buxmont Academy (CSF Buxmont) alternative school/day treatment program for troubled youth in eastern Pennsylvania.

A moving story about young people working to change their behavior and achieve their goals, the video is also instructive, showing a variety of restorative practices as they happen.

Building Our Community:
A Film about Restorative Practices

Building Our Community is a documentary about the positive impact of restorative practices at Collingwood Primary School, in Hull, UK, a city facing some of the most acute economic and social challenges in England. Once a school in crisis, through the adoption of restorative practices Collingwood built a highly positive school culture and an exceptional sense of community, and helped pupils develop skills to feel respected, happy and able to make the most of their lives.

This upbeat, informative video features interviews with teachers, students and parents sharing how they've benefited from the self-knowledge and empowerment developed during the restorative journey. The video is an engaging introduction to restorative practices in a school determined to give everyone a voice and a strong foundation for academic and emotional growth.

Four School Conferences:
A Composite View

Four actual Real Justice conferences were videotaped, with the permission of participants, at alternative schools operated by the Community Service Foundation and Buxmont Academy, sister nonprofit organizations serving troubled youth in eastern Pennsylvania. Footage from the conferences, which were held for offenses ranging from truancy and leaving school grounds to drug possession and bringing a knife onto a school bus, provide viewers with a realistic view of conferencing. Some conferences are highly emotional; others are not. Some conferences produce satisfying outcomes; others are less successful. But follow-up interviews with conference participants show that even a so-called "unsuccessful" conference can produce meaningful outcomes.

IIRP Globe Ball

This small, squeezable globe ball is perfect for use as a talking piece in restorative circles.

Restorative Questions Poster

This poster, designed for use in classrooms, prominently displays the essential restorative questions for easy reference in the event of a conflict or harmful incident. The top has questions used to respond to challenging behavior; the bottom has questions to help those harmed by others' actions. Dimensions: 18"w x 24"h.

Restorative Questions Sign

A rugged, portable A-frame sign, designed for use in schools and playgrounds, prominently displays the essential restorative questions for easy reference in the event of a conflict or harmful incident. One side has questions used to respond to challenging behavior; the other has questions to help those harmed by others' actions. Dimensions: 20"w x 35"h.

Restorative Questions Cards

This pack of 100 handy two-sided coated 2" x 3.5" cards puts the essential restorative questions at your fingertips. One side has questions used to respond to challenging behavior; the other has questions to help those harmed by others' actions. The cards fit easily in a wallet.

To learn more about books, videos and other resources provided by the IIRP, please go to **www.iirp.org/store**.

JOIN THE IIRP's RESTORATIVE PRACTICES eFORUM

To receive articles like the ones in this volume free via email, as well as those about restorative practices efforts in criminal justice, family and social services, and the workplace, join the IIRP's Restorative Practices eForum.

You'll receive occasional short emails including brief summaries of significant articles, research reports and information about upcoming restorative practices events — with links to full articles. Become part of a worldwide network of people who believe in the possibility of meaningful change.

eForum emails do not include attachments. We do not share our eForum database, so you will receive no spam.

Sign up at **www.iirp.org/eforum**.

About the IIRP

This volume is a publication of the International Institute for Restorative Practices (IIRP), the world's first graduate school wholly dedicated to the emerging field of restorative practices. The IIRP is engaged in the advanced education of professionals at the graduate level and to the conduct of research that can develop the growing field of restorative practices, with the goal of positively influencing human behavior and strengthening civil society throughout the world. The IIRP offers master's degree and certificate programs for educators and others who work with children and youth. To learn more about the IIRP Graduate School, go to **www.iirp.org**.

The IIRP Training and Consulting Division is the leading world provider of restorative practices training, consulting and international conferences, as well as print, video and other resources. The IIRP and its related organizations have trained thousands of individuals in education, criminal justice, and social and human services since its inception as the Real Justice program in 1995. To learn more about the IIRP Training and Consulting Division, go to **www.iirp.org/training**.